AFRICAN WRITERS SERIES   FOUNDING EDITOR Chinua Achebe

AFRICAN WRITERS SERIES

246

I Will Marry When I Want

J. Speran

Middlebury

1983

DEDICATION

To all those who have been at the forefront in the development of literature in Gĩkũyũ language through songs and books: Mũthĩrĩgũ and Mau Mau composers; contemporary composers like Kamaarũ, D. K. Kĩraatũ, Wahoome, Rũguĩti, Gathaithi Choir, Mwĩkũ Mwĩkũ Orchestra; and to all the other Kenyans who have been developing literature in all the other Kenya national languages through songs and books.

In particular, we can never forget the contribution of Gakaara wa Wanjaũ who long before the Mau Mau armed anti-imperialist struggle used to write books in Gĩkũyũ language. And even after Gakaara was detained by the British for his patriotic anti-imperialist literature, he never gave up his struggle to create a patriotic literature in Gĩkũyũ language. On being released from political detention, he continued to write and publish books and magazines in Gĩkũyũ:

All patriotic Kenyan writers, accept this, our offering!

I Will Marry When I Want

NGŨGĨ WA THIONG'O and
NGŨGĨ WA MĨRIĨ

Translated from the Gĩkũyũ by the authors

LONDON
HEINEMANN
IBADAN · NAIROBI

Heinemann Educational Books Ltd
22 Bedford Square, London WC1B 3HH
P.M.B. 5205 Ibadan · P.O. Box 45314 Nairobi

EDINBURGH   MELBOURNE   AUCKLAND
HONG KONG   SINGAPORE   KUALA LUMPUR   NEW DELHI
KINGSTON   PORT OF SPAIN

Heinemann Educational Books Inc.
4 Front Street, Exeter, New Hampshire 03833, U.S.A.

ISBN 0 435 90246 6

Set in Linotron Times by Willmer Brothers Limited, Birkenhead
Printed and bound in Great Britain by
Richard Clay (The Chaucer Press) Ltd., Bungay, Suffolk

I Will Marry When I Want

Characters

KĪGŪŪNDA, *Farm labourer*
WANGECI, *Kīgūūnda's wife*
GATHONI, *Their daughter*
GĪCAAMBA, *Kīgūūnda's neighbour, a factory worker*
NJOOKI, *Gīcaamba's wife*
AHAB KĪOI WA KANORU, *Wealthy farmer and businessman*
JEZEBEL, *Kīoi's wife*
SAMUEL NDUGĪRE, *Nouveau riche farmer and shopkeeper*
HELEN, *Ndugīre's wife*
IKUUA WA NDITIKA, *Kīoi's business partner*
DRUNK
WAITER
SECURICOR WATCHMAN

SINGERS, DANCERS, MUSICIANS, CHILDREN, WORKERS, MAU MAU
GUERRILLAS, BRITISH SOLDIERS, AFRICAN HOMEGUARDS

ACT ONE

*Kīgūūnda's home. A square, mud-walled, white-ochred, one-roomed
house. The white ochre is fading. In one corner can be seen Kīgūūnda
and Wangeci's bed. In another can be seen a pile of rags on the floor.
The floor is Gathoni's bed and the rags, her bedding. Although poorly
dressed,* GATHONI *is very beautiful. In the same room can be seen a pot
on three stones. On one of the walls there hangs a framed title-deed for
one and a half acres of land. Near the head of the bed, on the wall, there
hangs a sheathed sword. On one side of the wall there hangs
Kīgūūnda's coat, and on the opposite side, on the same wall,
Wangeci's coat. The coats are torn and patched. A pair of tyre sandals
and a basin can be seen on the floor.*

As the play opens, WANGECI *is just about to finish peeling potatoes.
She then starts to sort out the rice on a tray and engages in many other
actions to do with cooking.*

KĪGŪŪNDA *is mending the broken leg of a folding chair.* GATHONI *is
busy doing her hair. The atmosphere shows that they are waiting for
some guests. As* KĪGŪŪNDA *mends the chair, he accidentally causes the
title-deed to fall on the floor. He picks it up and gazes at it as if he is
spelling out the letters.*

WANGECI:
    What do you want to do with the title-deed?
    Why do you always gaze at it
    As if it was a title for a thousand acres?
KĪGŪŪNDA:
    These one and a half acres?
    These are worth more to me
    Than all the thousands that belong to Ahab Kīoi wa Kanoru.

> These are mine own,
> Not borrowed robes
> Said to tire the wearer.
> A man brags about his own penis,
> However tiny.

WANGECI:
> And will you be able to mend the chair in time
> Or are our guests to squat on the floor?

KĪGŪŪNDA: [*Laughing a little*]
> Ahab Kīoi son of Kanoru!
> And his wife Jezebel!
> To squat on the floor!

WANGECI:
> Go on then and
> Waste all the time in the world
> Gazing at the title-deed!

WANGECI *continues with her cooking chores.* KĪGŪŪNDA *puts the title-deed back on the wall, and resumes mending the chair. Suddenly drunk passes through the yard singing.*

DRUNK: [*Singing*]
> *I shall marry when I want,*
> *Since all padres are still alive.*
> *I shall get married when I want,*
> *Since all nuns are still alive.*

[*Near the door he stops and calls out*]
> Kīgūūnda wa Gathoni!
> Son of Mūrīma!
> Why didn't you come out for a drink?
> Or are you tied to your wife's petticoats?
> Do you suckle her?
> Come, let's go!

WANGECI: [*Runs to the door and shouts angrily*]
> Go away and drink that poisonous stuff at the bar!
> You wretch!
> Has alcohol become milk?
> Auuu-u!
> Have you no shame urinating there?

[*She looks for a stone or any other missile. But when she again looks out, she finds the drunk disappearing in the distance. She goes back to her seat by the fireplace*]

> He has gone away, legs astride the road,
> Doing I don't know what with his arms.
> Has drinking become work?
> Or have beer-halls become churches?

KĪGŪŪNDA:

> Was that not Kamande wa Mūnyui?
> Leave him alone,
> And don't look down upon him.
> He was a good man;
> He became the way he now is only after he lost his job.
> He worked with the Securicor company.
> He was Kīoi's nightwatchman.
> But one day Kīoi finds him dead asleep in the middle of the night.
> From that moment Kamande lost his job.
> Before the Securicor company he was an administrative
>   policeman.
> That's why when he takes one too many,
> He swings his arms about as if he is carrying a gun.

WANGECI:

> Alcohol will now employ him!

KĪGŪŪNDA:

> Poverty has no heroes,
> He who judges knows not how he will be judged!

Suddenly a hymn breaks out in the yard. KĪGŪŪNDA *stops work and listens.* WANGECI *listens for a little while, then she continues with her activities.* GATHONI *goes out into the yard where the singers are.*

SOLOIST:

> *The Satan of poverty*
> *Must be crushed!*

CHORUS:

> *Hallelujah he must be crushed,*
> *For the second coming is near.*

SOLOIST:

> *He destroys our homes,*
> *Let's crush him.*

CHORUS:
> *Hallelujah let's crush him and grind him*
> *For the second coming is near.*

SOLOIST:
> *The Satan of theft*
> *Must be crushed!*

CHORUS:
> *Hallelujah he must be crushed,*
> *For the second coming is near.*

SOLOIST:
> *Crush and cement him to the ground,*
> *Crush him!*

CHORUS:
> *Hallelujah crush and cement him to the ground,*
> *For the second coming is near.*

SOLOIST:
> *He oppresses the whole nation,*
> *Let's crush him!*

CHORUS:
> *Hallelujah let's crush and grind him,*
> *For the second coming is near.*

SOLOIST:
> *The Satan of robbery*
> *Must be crushed!*

CHORUS:
> *Hallelujah he must be crushed,*
> *For the second coming is near.*

SOLOIST:
> *Bury him and plant thorn trees on the grave.*

CHORUS:
> *Bury him and plant thorn trees on the grave,*
> *For the second coming is near.*

SOLOIST:
> *He brings famine to our children,*
> *Let's crush him!*

CHORUS:
> *Hallelujah let's crush and grind him,*
> *For the second coming is near.*

SOLOIST:

> *The Satan of oppression*
> *Must be crushed!*

CHORUS:

> *Hallelujah he must be crushed,*
> *For the second coming is near.*

SOLOIST:

> *Crush and cement him to the ground,*
> *Crush him!*

CHORUS:

> *Hallelujah crush and cement him to the ground,*
> *Crush him!*

SOLOIST:

> *He holds back our rising awareness*
> *Let's crush him.*

CHORUS:

> *Hallelujah let's crush and grind him,*
> *For the second coming is near.*

SOLOIST:

> *Our people let's sing in unity,*
> *And crush him!*

CHORUS:

> *Hallelujah let's crush and grind him,*
> *For the second coming is near.*

SOLOIST:

> *I can't hear your voices*
> *Let's crush him!*

CHORUS:

> *Hallelujah let's crush and grind him,*
> *For the second coming is near . . .*

The group LEADER *now enters* KĪGŪŪNDA*'s house and stands by the door holding a container for subscriptions.* GATHONI *also enters and stands where she had previously sat.*

LEADER:

> Praise the Lord!

KĪGŪŪNDA
WANGECI } [*Looking at one another as if unable to know what to say*]

> We are well,

And you too we hope.

LEADER:

We belong to the sect of the poor.
Those without land,
Those without plots,
Those without clothes.
We want to put up our own church.
We have a haraambe.*
Give generously to the God of the poor
Whatever you have put aside
To ward off the fate of Anania and his wife.

KĪGŪŪNDA: [*Making a threatening step or two towards the* LEADER]
We can hardly afford to feed our bellies.
You think we can afford any for haraambe?

The LEADER *goes out quickly. The group resumes their song.*

SOLOIST:

The devil of stinginess
Must be crushed!

CHORUS:

Hallelujah let's crush him
And press him to the ground,
For the second coming is near.

SOLOIST:

He is making it difficult for us to build churches,
Let's crush him!

CHORUS:

Hallelujah let's crush him and press him down,
For the second coming is near.

SOLOIST:

The devil of darkness
Must be crushed . . .

KĪGŪŪNDA: [*Rushing to the door*]
Take away your hymn from my premises
Take it away to the bush!

---

*Haraambe: Public fund-raising

They go away, their voices fading in the distance. GATHONI *sits down and resumes doing her hair.*

KĪGŪŪNDA:
>That we build a church in honour of poverty!
>Poverty!
>Even if poverty was to sell at five cents,
>I would never buy it!
>Religions in this village will drive us all crazy!
>Night and day!
>You are invited to a haraambe fund-raising for the church.
>Which church?
>Of the White Padre and Virgin Mary.
>You are invited to a haraambe for the church.
>Which church?
>Of the P.C.E.A* The Scottish one.
>Haraambe for the church.
>Which church?
>Of the Anglicans.
>Of the Greek Orthodox.
>Of Kikuyu Independent.
>Of Salvation Army.
>Of the Sect of Deep Waters.
>Are we the rubbish heap of religions?
>So that wherever the religions are collected,
>They are thrown in our courtyard?
>And now the sect of the poor?
>Religion, religion, religion!
>Haraambe, haraambe, haraambe!
>And those church buildings are only used once a week!
>Or is this another profitable business?

WANGECI:
>You know they were here the other day
>Trying to convert me!

---

*P.C.E.A.: Presbyterian Church of East Africa

KĪGŪŪNDA:
> Who? The same lot?

WANGECI:
> What do they call themselves?
> The ones that came from America very recently,
> Those ones: their haraambe is not local
> They say you take them a tenth
> Of all you earn or harvest.
> Even if it's a tenth of the maize or beans
> You have grown in your small shamba* . . .

KĪGŪŪNDA:
> All that haraambe,
> To America.

WANGECI:
> What are they called now?

KĪGŪŪNDA: [*Pretending anger at her*]
> And why don't you follow them
> To Rome, Greece or that America
> Singing [*Sings in mimicry*]
> *The devil must be crushed,*
> *Crush him!*
> *For darkness is falling . . .*

[WANGECI *and* GATHONI *laugh*]

WANGECI:
> That voice of yours attempting foreign songs
> Could frighten a baby into tears:

KĪGŪŪNDA: [*Suddenly seized by a lighthearted mood*]
> This voice that belongs to Kīgūūnda wa Gathoni?
> Don't you remember before the Emergency†
> How I used to sing and dance the Mūcūng'wa dance?
> Was it not then that you fell in love with these shapely legs?

---

*Shamba: farm
†Emergency: Kenya was under a British imposed State of Emergency from 1952 to 1962

WANGECI:
>   You, able to dance to Mũcũng'wa?

KĨGŨŨNDA:
>   Gathoni,
>   Bring me that sword on the wall.

[GATHONI *goes for the sword*]
>   I want to show this woman
>   How I then used to do it!

GATHONI *hands the sword to* KĨGŨŨNDA. KĨGŨŨNDA *ties the sword round his waist. He starts the Mũcũng'wa. In his head he begins to see the vision of how they used to dance the Mũcũng'wa. Actual* DANCERS *now appear on the stage led by* KĨGŨŨNDA *and his wife.*

KĨGŨŨNDA: [*Soloist*]
>   *I am he on whom it rained*
>   *As I went up and down*
>   *The Mũitĩrĩri mountain.*

DANCERS:
>   *I am he on whom it rained*
>   *As I went up and down*
>   *TheMũitĩrĩri mountain.*

KĨGŨŨNDA:
>   *I was late and far away from home*
>   *I spent the night in a maiden's bed*
>   *My mother said they should go back for me*
>   *My father said they should not go back for me.*

DANCERS:
>   *I was late and far away from home*
>   *I spent the night in a maiden's bed*
>   *My mother said they should go back for me*
>   *My father said they should not go back for me.*

KĨGŨŨNDA:
>   *Maiden lend me your precious treasures*
>   *And I will lend you my precious treasures*
>   *Maiden, the treasures I'll lend you*

> Will make you lose your head
> And when you lose your head you'll never find it again.

DANCERS:

> Maiden lend me your precious treasures
> And I will lend you my precious treasures
> Maiden, the treasures I'll lend you
> Will make you lose your head
> And when you lose your head you'll never find it again.

KĪGŪŪNDA:

> Whose homestead is this
> Where my voice is now raised in song,
> Where once my mother refused a marriage offer
> And I wetted the bed?

DANCERS:

> Whose homestead is this
> Where my voice is now raised in song,
> Where once my mother refused a marriage offer
> And I wetted the bed?

KĪGŪŪNDA:

> My mother's bridewealth was a calf taken in battle,
> The calf was tended by young warriors.
> Many hands make work light.

DANCERS:

> My mother's bridewealth was a calf taken in battle,
> The calf was tended by young warriors.
> Many hands make work light.

KĪGŪŪNDA:

> Mother ululate for me,
> For if I don't die young I'll one day sing songs of victory.
> Oh, yes, come what come may
> If I don't die young I'll one day sing songs of victory.

DANCERS:

> Mother ululate for me,
> For if I don't die young I'll one day sing songs of victory.
> Oh, yes, come what come may
> If I don't die young I'll one day sing songs of victory.

KĪGŪŪNDA:

> The crown of victory should be taken away from traitors

> And be handed back to patriots
> Like Kīmaathi's* patriotic heroes.

DANCERS:
> The crown of victory should be taken away from traitors
> And be handed back to patriots
> Like Kīmaathi's patriotic heroes.

All the DANCERS *leave the arena.* KĪGŪŪNDA *goes on alone and repeats the last verse.*

KĪGŪŪNDA:
> The crown of victory should be taken away from traitors
> And be handed back to patriots
> Like Kīgūūnda wa Gathoni . . .

WANGECI: [*Cutting him short*]
> Sit down!
> An aging hero has no admirers!

[*Kīgūūnda unties the sword and hangs it back on the wall*]
> Who prevented you from selling out?
> Today we would be seeing you
> In different models of Mercedez Benzes,
> With stolen herds of cows and sheep,
> With huge plantations,
> With servants to look after your massive properties.
> Yes, like all the other men around!
> They are now the ones employing you,
> Jobs without wages!
> Hurry up and mend that chair,
> Kīoi and his family are about to arrive.
> Hasn't that chair been in that condition all this time,
> Without you doing anything about it?
> If they arrive this very minute,
> Where will they sit?

KĪGŪŪNDA: [*Hurrying up with the work. When he finishes repairing it, he sits on it, trying to see if it's firm*]
> What can they do to me even if they enter this minute?

---

*Dedan Kīmaathi: Mau Mau guerrilla leader

Let them come with their own chairs
Those spring and sponge ones that seem to fart
As you sink into them.
[*He sings as if he is asking* WANGECI *a question*]
Whose homestead is this?
Whose homestead is this?
Whose homestead is this?
So that I can roll on the dust
Like the calf of a buffalo!

KĪGŪŪNDA *waits for an answer.* WANGECI *merely glances at him for
about a second and then continues with her work.* KĪGŪŪNDA *now sings
as if he is answering himself. Still singing, he stands up and walks to the
title-deed, pulls it off the wall and looks at it.*
This is mine own homestead
This is mine own homestead
This is mine own homestead
If I want to roll on the dust
I am free to do so.

WANGECI:
I wonder what Mr Kīoi
And Jezebel, his madam,
Want in a poor man's home?
Why did they take all that trouble to let us know beforehand
That they would be coming here today?

KĪGŪŪNDA:
You, you woman,
Even if you see me in these tatters
I am not poor.
[*He shows her the title-deed by pointing at it. Then he hangs it back on
the wall*]
You should know
That a man without debts is not poor at all.
Aren't we the ones who make them rich?
Were it not for my blood and sweat
And the blood and sweat of all the other workers,
Where would the likes of Kīoi and his wife now be?
Tell me!
Where would they be today?

WANGECI:

> Leave me alone,
> You'll keep on singing the same song
> Till the day you people wake up.
> A fool's walking stick supports the clever.
> But why do you sit idle
> While this bedframe
> Also needs a nail or two?

KĪGŪŪNDA *takes the hammer and goes to repair the bed.* WANGECI *turns her face and sees* GATHONI's *bedding on the floor.*

> Gathoni, Gathoni!

GATHONI:

> Yes!

WANGECI:

> Gathoni!

GATHONI:

> Yeees!

WANGECI:

> Can't you help me
> In peeling potatoes,
> In sorting out the rice,
> Or in looking after the fire?
> Instead of sitting there,
> Legs stretched,
> Plaiting your hair?

GATHONI:

> Mother you love complaining
> Haven't I just swept the floor?

WANGECI:

> And what is that bedding doing over there?
> Can't you put it somewhere in a corner,
> Or else take it outside to the sun
> So the fleas can fly away?

GATHONI:

> These tatters!
> Are these what you call bedding?
> And this floor,
> Is this what you call a bed?

WANGECI:

> Why don't you get yourself a husband
> Who'll buy you spring beds?

GATHONI:

> Mother, why are you insulting me?
> Is that why you refused to send me to school,
> So that I may remain your slave,
> And for ever toil for you?
> Picking tea and coffee only for you to pocket the wages?
> And all that so that you can get money
> To pay fees for your son!
> Do you want me to remain buried under these ashes?
> And on top of all that injury
> You have to abuse me night and day?
> Do you think I cannot get a husband?
> I'll be happy the day I leave this home!

WANGECI: [*With sarcasm*]

> Take to the road!
> There's no girl worth the name
> Who is contented with being an old maid
> In her mother's homestead.

GATHONI:

> Sorry!
> I shall marry when I want.
> Nobody will force me into it!

WANGECI:

> What? What did you say?

GATHONI:

> I shall marry when I want.

WANGECI:

> You dare talk back to me like that?
> Oh, my clansmen, come!
> You have started to insult me at your age?
> Why don't you wait until you have grown some teeth!

[*With sarcasm*]

> You! Let me warn you.
> If I was not expecting some guests
> I would teach you never to abuse your mother.

Take these potato peelings and throw them out in the yard.
[GATHONI *takes the peelings. As she is about to go out, her father shouts at her*]

KĪGŪŪNDA:

Gathoni!
[GATHONI *looks at her father fearfully*]
Come here.
[GATHONI *makes only one step forward still in fear*]

If ever I see or hear that again . . .!
Utaona cha mtema kuni.
Do you think that we mine gold,
To enable us to educate boys and girls?
Go away!
Na uchunge mdomo wako.
[GATHONI *takes the peelings out*]

WANGECI:

What's wrong with the child?
She used not to be like this!

KĪGŪŪNDA:

It's all the modern children.
They have no manners at all.
In my time
We could not even sneeze in front of our parents.
What they need is a whip
To make them straighten up!

WANGECI:

No!
When children get to that age,
We can only watch them and hope for the best.
When axes are kept in one basket they must necessarily knock
    against each other.
She'll soon marry and be out of sight.
There's no maiden who makes a home in her father's backyard.
And there's no maiden worth the name who wants to get grey
    hairs at her parents' home.

KĪGŪŪNDA:

Do modern girls marry,
Or do they only go to the bars

Accompanied by men old enough to be their fathers,
And the girls cooing up to them, sugardaddy, sugardaddy!
Even for those who have gone to school up to secondary
Or up to the Makerere grade of Cambridge
The song is still the same!
Sugardaddy, sugardaddy!

GATHONI *enters and goes back to where she was before and continues with doing her hair as if she is getting ready to go out*

WANGECI:
    Have you gone back to your hair?
    What's wrong with this child!
    Bring me the salt.

[GATHONI *brings soda ash instead*]
    Oh, clansmen, did I ask you for soda ash?

GATHONI:
    I did not find any salt.

WANGECI:
    So you suggest we put soda ash in the stew?
    Look for the salt.

GATHONI:
    There is no salt.
    Wasn't it finished last night?

WANGECI:
    Where shall I now turn?
    Give me some money so Gathoni can run for salt!

KĪGŪŪNDA: [*Searches his pockets*]
    I have no money. I gave it all to you.
    Didn't you buy cooking oil, rice and salt?

WANGECI:
    Thirty cents' worth of cooking oil
    And half a kilo of sugar!
    Was that all that exhausted your pockets?

KĪGŪŪNDA:
    The given does not know when the granary is empty.
    Do you think that taking out is the same thing as banking?

WANGECI:
    He who puts on dancing finery knows how he is going to dance in
        the arena!

You were the one who said that we should cook food for the
   visitors, not so?

KĪGŪŪNDA: [*Not happy with the subject, trying to change it*]
   Do you know that in the past,
   The amount of money I gave you
   Would have bought more than three kilos of sugar?
   Today, am I expected to cut myself to pieces
   Or to increase my salary by force
   To enable me to keep abreast with the daily increase in prices?
   Didn't they increase the price of flour only yesterday?

WANGECI: [*Sarcastically*]
   The difference between then and now is this!
   We now have our independence!

KĪGŪŪNDA:
   I ran away from coldland only to find myself in frostland!

WANGECI:
   But even if prices rise
   Without the wages rising,
   Or even if there are no jobs,
   Are we expected to eat saltless food?
   Or do they want us to use ashes?
   Gathoni!

GATHONI:
   Yees.

WANGECI:
   Can you run over to Gīcaamba's place
   And ask them for some salt!
   Those are never without anything
   Because of their fortnightly pay.

[GATHONI *begins to move*]
   And Gathoni!

GATHONI:
   Yees.

WANGECI:
   And . . . eem . . . and . . . eem,
   Don't tell them that we have guests.
   This food cannot feed guests
   And feed the whole village.

[GATHONI *goes out*]

KĪGŪŪNDA: [*As if his thoughts are still on wages and price increases*]
>You talk about prices,
>But tell me a single item whose price has not gone up?
>In the past a mere thirty shillings,
>Could buy me clothes and shoes,
>And enough flour for my belly.
>Today I get two hundred shillings a month,
>And it can't even buy insecticide enough to kill a single bedbug.
>African employers are no different
>From Indian employers
>Or from the Boer white landlords.
>They don't know the saying
>That the hand of a worker should not be weakened.
>They don't know the phrase, 'increased wages'!

WANGECI:
>Are we the pot that cooks without eating?

GATHONI *enters panting. It looks as if she has something on her mind.*

GATHONI:
>We have been given a lot of salt!

Before GATHONI *sits down a car hoots from the road.* GATHONI *does not know if she should sit down or run out, she shuffles about doubtfully.*

WANGECI:
>What kind of a person is this?
>He never enters the house to greet people!

[*The car hoots again, now with more force and impatience*]

WANGECI:
>Go, you are the one being called out by John Mūhūūni.
>Why don't you get out before he makes us deaf with the hooting

[GATHONI *goes out*]
>Do you know that Gathoni began to be difficult
>Only after this son of Kīoi started this business of hooting for
>   her?

[KĪGŪŪNDA *goes on with his work as if he has not heard anything*]
>The son of Kīoi!
>What does he want with Gathoni?
>Gathoni being a child,

Does she realize that men have prickly needles!

KĪGŪŪNDA:

You should have said that it is the modern men
Who have got prickly needles.
Give me water to wash my feet.

WANGECI *brings him water in a basin.* KĪGŪŪNDA *goes and gets his tyre sandals from the floor. He now imitates the gait of young men as he walks towards the basin talking all the time.*

Modern young men?
You can never tell!
Ask them to put on bell bottoms
And to put on platform shoes,
And then to whistle whistles of hypocrisy,
That's all they are able to do.
But it has well been said that
The father and mother of the beautiful one have no ears.

WANGECI: [*Starts as if an idea has suddenly occurred to her*]
Could it be the reason why . . .?

KĪGŪŪNDA:

Why what?

WANGECI:

Mūhūūni's father and mother, Kīoi and Jezebel, are visiting us?
They have never before wanted to visit us!

KĪGŪŪNDA:

To visit, yes – to say what?

WANGECI:

It could be that . . .

KĪGŪŪNDA:

You women!
You are always thinking of weddings!

WANGECI:

Why not?
These are different times from ours.
These days they sing that love knows no fear.
In any case, can't you see
Your daughter is very beautiful?
She looks exactly the way I used to look – a perfect beauty!

KĪGŪŪNDA: [*Stopping dusting up the tyre sandals*]
>   You? A perfect beauty?

WANGECI:
>   Yes. Me.

KĪGŪŪNDA:
>   Don't you know that it was only that
>   I felt pity for you?

WANGECI:
>   You, who used to waylay me everywhere all the time?
>   In the morning,
>   In the evening,
>   As I came home from the river,
>   As I came home from the market,
>   Or as I came back home from work in the settlers' farms?
>   Can't you remember how you used to plead with me,
>   Saying you had never in your life seen a beauty like me?

KĪGŪŪNDA: [*Going back in time*]
>   That was long before the state of Emergency.
>   Your heels used to shine bright,
>   Your face shone like the clear moon at night,
>   Your eyes like the stars in heaven.
>   Your teeth, it seemed, were always washed with milk.
>   Your voice sounded like a precious instrument.
>   Your breasts were full and pointed like the tip of the sharpest
>   thorn.
>   As you walked it seemed as if they were whistling beautiful
>   tunes.

WANGECI: [*Also mesmerized by memories of their past youth*]
>   In those days
>   We used to dance in Kīneenii forest.

KĪGŪŪNDA:
>   A dance would cost only twenty-five cents.

WANGECI:
>   In those days there was not a single girl from Ndeiya up to
>   Gīthīīga
>   Who did not die to dance with you.

KĪGŪŪNDA:

> You too would swing your skirt
> Till the guitar player was moved to breaking the strings.
> And the guitars used to sound tunes
> That silenced the entire forest,
> Making even the trees listen . . .

The sound of guitars and other instruments as if KĪGŪŪNDA *and* WANGECI *can hear them in the memory.* KĪGŪŪNDA *and* WANGECI *start dancing. Then they are joined by the guitar players and players of other instruments and* DANCERS. *They dance,* KĪGŪŪNDA *and* WANGECI *among them.*

> *Nyaangwīcū let's shake the skirt*
> *Nyaangwīcū let's shake the skirt*
> *Sister shake it and make it yield its precious yields.*
> *Sister shake it and make it yield its precious yields.*
>
> *Nyaangwīcū is danced on one leg*
> *Nyaangwīcū is danced on one leg*
> *The other is merely for pleasing the body.*
> *The other is merely for pleasing the body.*
>
> *Wangeci the beautiful one*
> *Wangeci the beautiful one*
> *With a body slim and straight like the eucalyptus.*
> *With a body slim and straight like the eucalyptus.*
>
> *Wangeci the little maiden*
> *Wangeci the little maiden*
> *When I see her I am unable to walk.*
> *When I see her I am unable to walk.*
>
> *Wangeci let's cultivate the fruit garden*
> *Wangeci let's cultivate the fruit garden*
> *This garden that belongs to Kīgūūnda wa Gathoni.*
> *This garden that belongs to Kīgūūnda wa Gathoni.*

Wangeci, our mother, we now refuse
Wangeci, our mother, we now refuse
To be slaves in our home,
To be slaves in our home.

When this is over, WANGECI *says. 'Oh my favourite was Mwomboko.'*
And KĪGŪŪNDA *replies: 'Oh in those days we used to tear the right or left*
side of trouser legs from the knee downwards. Those were our bell
bottoms with which we danced Mwomboko.' Now the guitar players
and the accordion players start. The Mwomboko DANCERS *enter.*
KĪGŪŪNDA *and* WANGECI *lead them in the Mwomboko dance. Guitars,*
iron rings and the accordions are played with vigour and the dancers'
feet add embellishments.

The Mwomboko dance is not difficult,
It's just two steps and a turn.
I'll swing you so beautifully that,
Your mother being in the fields,
Your father in a beer feast,
You'll tell me where your father's purse is hidden.
> *Take care of me*
> *I take care of you*
> *Problems can be settled in jokes.*
Limuru is my home
Here I have come to loaf about
Wangeci, my young lady
Be the way you are
And don't add frills
To your present gait.
> *Take care of me*
> *I take care of you*
> *Problems can be settled in jokes.*
This is your place
Famed for ripe bananas
I'll sing to you till you cry
Or failing to cry
You'll be so overcome with feelings

> *That you'll take your life.*
>> *Take care of me*
>> *I take care of you*
>> *Problems can be settled in jokes.*
> *I brewed liquor for you*
> *And now you've turned against me!*
> *A cripple often turns against his benefactors*
> *Our son of Gathoni*
> *Good fortune, unexpected, found Wacū in the Field*
> *And she sat down to feast on it.*
>> *Take care of me*
>> *I take care of you*
>> *Problems can be settled in jokes.*
> *Have you taken one too many*
> *Or are you simply drunk*
> *I'll not say anything,*
> *Oh, Wangeci my little fruit,*
> *Until seven years are over . . .*

The voices of men and the sound of guitars, accordions and other instruments end abruptly. The DANCERS *leave the stage.* KĪGŪŪNDA *and* WANGECI *remain frozen in the act of dancing.* KĪGŪŪNDA *shakes his head as if he is still engrossed in memories of the past. They disengage slowly!*

KĪGŪŪNDA:
> Oh, the seven years were not even over
> When we began
> To sing new songs with new voices,
> Songs and voices demanding
> Freedom for Kenya, our motherland.

A procession enters the stage singing freedom songs.

> *Freedom*
> *Freedom*
> *Freedom for Kenya our motherland*

A land of limitless joy
A land rich in green fields and forests
Kenya is an African people's country.

We do not mind being jailed
We do not mind being exiled
For we shall never never stop
Agitating for and demanding back our lands
For Kenya is an African people's country . . .

As the SINGERS *leave the stage* WANGECI *takes over the remembrance of things past.*

WANGECI:
          I myself have always remembered
          The Olengurueni women,
          The ones driven from their lands around Nakuru
          To be exiled to Yatta, the land of black rocks.
          They passed through Limuru
          Caged with barbed wire in the backs of several lorries.
          But still they sang songs
          With words that pierced one's heart like a spear.
          The songs were sad, true,
          But the women were completely fearless
          For they had faith and were sure that,
          One day, this soil will be returned to us.

A procession of women SINGERS *enter the stage singing.*

          Pray in Truth
          Beseech Him with Truth
          For he is the same Ngai* within us.
          One woman died
          After being tortured
          Because she refused to sell out.

---

*Ngai: God

> *Pray in Truth*
> *Beseech Him with Truth*
> *For he is the same Ngai within us.*
> *Great love I found there*
> *Among women and children*
> *A bean fell to the ground*
> *And it was shared among them.*
> *Pray in Truth*
> *Beseech Him with Truth*
> *For he is the same Ngai within us.*

The SINGERS *leave the stage.*

KĪGŪŪNDA:
> It was then
> That the state of Emergency was declared over Kenya.
> Our patriots,
> Men and women of
> Limuru and the whole country,
> Were arrested!
> The Emergency laws became very oppressive.
> Our homes were burnt down.
> We were jailed,
> We were taken to detention camps,
> Some of us were crippled through beatings.
> Others were castrated.
> Our women were raped with bottles.
> Our wives and daughters raped before our eyes!

[*Moved by the bitter memories,* KĪGŪŪNDA *pauses for few seconds*]
> But through Mau Mau
> Led by Kĩmaathi and Matheenge,
> And through the organized unity of the masses
> We beat the whites
> And freedom came . . .
> We raised high our national flag.

A jubilant procession of men, women and children enters the stage singing songs and dances in praise of freedom.

It is a flag of three colours
Raise the flag high
Green is for our earth
Raise the flag high
Red is for our blood
Raise the flag high
Black is for Africa
Raise the flag high.
[*They change to a new song and dance*]
SOLOIST:
Great our patriots for me . . .
Where did the whites come from?
CHORUS:
Where did the whites come from?
Where did the whites come from?
They came through Mūrang'a,
And they spent a night at Waiyaki's home,
If you want to know that these foreigners were no good,
Ask yourself:
Where is Waiyaki's grave today?
We must protect our patriots
So they don't meet Waiyaki's fate.
SOLOIST:
Kīmaathi's patriots are brave
Where did the whites come from?
[*They continue singing as they walk off the stage.*]
KĪGŪŪNDA:
How the times run!
How many years have gone
Since we got independence?
Ten and over,
Quite a good number of years!
And now look at me!
[KĪGŪŪNDA *looks at himself, points to the title-deed and goes near it*]
One and a half acres of land in dry plains.
Our family land was given to homeguards.
Today I am just a labourer

On farms owned by Ahab Kīoi wa Kanoru.
My trousers are pure tatters.
Look at you.
See what the years of freedom in poverty
Have done to you!
Poverty has hauled down your former splendour.
Poverty has dug trenches on your face,
Your heels are now so many cracks,
Your breasts have fallen,
They have nowhere to hold.
Now you look like an old basket
That has lost all shape.

WANGECI:
Away with you,
Haven't you heard it said that
A flower is robbed of the colours by the fruit it bears!
[*Changing the tone of voice*]
Stop this habit of thinking too much about the past
Often losing your sleep over things that had better be forgotten.
Think about today and tomorrow.
Think about our home.
Poverty has no permanent roots!
Poverty is a sword for sharpening the digging sticks . . .
[*Pauses, as if caught by a new thought*]
Tell me:
What does Kīoi and his family
Want with us today?

KĪGŪŪNDA:
Well, they want to see how their slave lives!
To see his bed for instance!

WANGECI:
Of all the years you have worked there,
Is it only now that they have realized you have a home?

KĪGŪŪNDA: [*Lightheartedly*]
They want . . . to come . . . to tell you . . . that . . .
You must tell . . . your daughter . . . to stop . . .
Going places with their son!

WANGECI:
>   Yes, for I myself did not feel birth pangs for Gathoni?
>   Should they dare to say such a thing,
>   I'll make them tell me whether it's Gathoni
>   Who goes to hoot a car outside their home day and night.

KĪGŪŪNDA: [*Suddenly remembering something*]
>   Wait a minute!

WANGECI:
>   What is it?

KĪGŪŪNDA *puts his hands in his pockets, obviously searching for something. He takes out a letter. He reads it silently. Then he goes to where the title-deed is and pulls it off.*

WANGECI: [*Repeating the question*] What is it?

KĪGŪŪNDA:
>   You know the rich fellow
>   They call Ikuua wa Nditika?

WANGECI:
>   The great friend of Kīoi?

KĪGŪŪNDA:
>   Yes. That's the one.
>   It's really true that a rich man
>   Can even dig up forbidden sacred shrines!
>   He wrote me this letter
>   And told me that there is a company
>   Belonging to some foreigners from America, Germany
>   And from that other country, yes, Japan,
>   Which wants to build a factory
>   For manufacturing insecticide
>   For killing bedbugs!
>   They want to buy my one and half acres
>   For they say the plot is well situated in a dry flat plain
>   And yet very near a railway line!
>   Ikuua wa Nditika and Kīoi wa Kanoru
>   Are the local directors of the company.
>   It's therefore possible that Kīoi is coming
>   To talk over the matter with me.

WANGECI:
> Stop. Stop it there.
> Aren't they the real bedbugs,
> Local watchmen for foreign robbers?
> When they see a poor man's property their mouths water,
> When they get their own, their mouths dry up!
> Don't they have any lands
> They can share with these foreigners
> Whom they have invited back into the country
> To desecrate the land?

A knock at the door. KĪGŪŪNDA *quickly hangs back the title-deed and puts the letter back into his pocket.* WANGECI *runs about putting things straight here and there for she thinks that* KĪOI *and his family have arrived. She exclaims: 'They have come and the food is not yet ready!' Another knock.* GĪCAAMBA *and* NJOOKI *enter. They are a worker and his peasant wife and they look mature in mind and body.* GĪCAAMBA *is dressed in overalls.* KĪGŪŪNDA *and* WANGECI *are obviously disappointed.*

KĪGŪŪNDA ⎫
WANGECI ⎬ : So it's you?

GĪCAAMBA ⎫
NJOOKI ⎬ : Yes . . . How are you?

WANGECI ⎫
KĪGŪŪNDA ⎬ : We are well.

NJOOKI:
> Give us what you have cooked.

WANGECI:
> The food is still cooking.

KĪGŪŪNDA:
> Karibu*, karibu.

WANGECI:
> Aren't you sitting down?

---

*Karibu: welcome

GĪCAAMBA *takes a chair.* KĪGŪŪNDA *also takes a chair near* GĪCAAMBA.
*They sit in such a way that the men are able to talk to one another, and
the two women the same.*

NJOOKI: [*To* WANGECI]

Gathoni told us that you had visitors.
And so I asked myself,
Who are these secret guests?
Could they be whites from abroad?
And you know very well a white has no favourite?

WANGECI:

Gathoni is too quick with her tongue.
It's Kīoi and his family
Who said they would like to pass by
On their way from the church.

NJOOKI:

Just passing by? I wonder.
Since when have rich men been known to visit their servants?

WANGECI:

We don't know what they really want.
In fact you found us asking ourselves the same question.
They sent a word the day before yesterday.
Even their son, John Mūhūūni,
Has just come for Gathoni this very minute.
He is a real particle of Godhead.
But he hardly ever talks with people.
He, for instance, never enters the house.
He just hoots and whistles from the road.

NJOOKI:

Let me caution you for even a wise man can be taught wisdom.
Ask Gathoni to cut off that relationship.
Rich families marry from rich families,
The poor from the poor!
Can't you see that the children of the big men,
And of these others who brag that they are mature men
All go to big houses!
Or have you become Jesus-is-my-saviour converts
And I have never heard you shouting 'Praise the Lord!'
And giving testimony . . .

KĪGŪŪNDA:
>   . . . but you are slightly better off,
>   For you are paid every fortnight.

GĪCAAMBA:
>   Even though we are paid fortnightly
>   Wages can never equal the work done.
>   Wages can never really compensate for your labour.
>   Gīkūyū* said:
>   If you want to rob a monkey of a baby it is holding
>   You must first throw it a handful of peanuts.
>   We the workers are like that monkey
>   When they want to steal our labour
>   They bribe us with a handful of peanuts.
>   We are the people who cultivate and plant
>   But we are not the people who harvest!
>   The owners of these companies are real scorpions.
>   They know three things only:
>   To oppress workers,
>   To take away their rights,
>   And to suck their blood.

The two women stop their own chatter to listen to GĪCAAMBA. GĪCAAMBA
*speaks with a conviction that shows that he has thought deeply about
these matters. He uses a lot of movement, gestures, mimicry, miming,
imitation, impersonation, any and every dramatic device to convey his
message.*

GĪCAAMBA:
>   Look at me.
>   It's Sunday.
>   I'm on my way to the factory.
>   This company has become my God.
>   That's how we live.
>   You wake up before dawn.
>   You rub your face with a bit of water
>   Just to remove dirt from the eyes!

---

*Gīkūyū: name of the founder of the Gīkūyū nationality but in this
  context means personification of the whole community.

Before you have drunk a cup of milkless tea,
The Sirena cries out.
You dash out.
Another siren.
You jump to the machine.
You sweat and sweat and sweat.
Another siren.
It's lunch break.
You find a corner with your plain grains of maize.
But before you have had two mouthfuls,
Another siren,
The lunch break is over.
Go back to the machine.
You sweat and sweat and sweat.
Siren.
It's six o'clock, time to go home.
Day in, day out,
Week after week!
A fortnight is over.
During that period
You have made shoes worth millions.
You are given a mere two hundred shillings,
The rest is sent to Europe.
Another fortnight.
You are on night shift.
You leave your wife's sweat.
Now you are back at the machine.
You sweat and sweat and sweat,
You sweat the whole night.
In the morning you go home.
You are drunk with sleep.
Your wife has already gone to the fields.
You look for the food.
Before you have swallowed two mouthfuls,
You are dead asleep.
You snore and snore.
Evening is here!

You meet your wife returning from the fields.
Bye, bye,
You tell her as you run to the machine.
Sweat.
Another fortnight.
Here, take this
Two hundred shillings.
The rest to Europe.
By that time you have sold away
Your body,
Your blood,
Your wife,
Even your children!
Why, because you hardly ever see them!
There are some who sell away their blood,
And they end up dying in there.
But many more end up as cripples.
Remember the son of . . . eeeh . . . you know who I mean . . .
The chemical dust
Accumulated in his body
Until the head cracked!
Did they take him to hospital?
Oh, no.
Was he given any compensation?
He was summarily dismissed, instead.
What about the son of . . . eeh . . .
You know the K.C.A.* elder? The one
Who, with others, started the freedom struggle? . . .
His son used to work in the cementing section
Where they keep retex and other dangerous chemicals.
The chemicals and the dust accumulated in his body,
He was forced to go to the Aga Khan Hospital for an operation.
What did they find inside him? A stone.
But was it a stone or a mountain!

K.C.A.: Kikuyu Central Assocation, a militant political movement.

It was a mountain made of those chemicals!
He was summarily retired with twenty-five cents as
    compensation.
What has life now got to offer him?
Is he not already in his grave though still breathing?
Since I was employed in that factory,
Twenty-one people in that section have died.
Yes, twenty-one people!

KĪGŪŪNDA:

Oooh, this is a very serious matter!
If I were to be told to work in that retex section
I, son of Gathoni,
Would then and there part ways with that company.

GĪCAAMBA:

I wouldn't mind, son of Gathoni,
If after selling away our labour,
Our village had benefited.
But look now at this village!
When was this company established?
Before the Second World War.
What did it bring into the country?
A few machines,
And money for erecting buildings to house the machines.
Where did they get the land on which to build?
Here!
Where did they get the charcoal for use by the machine?
Here!
Was it not this factory together with the railways
Which swallowed up all the forests around?
Is that not why today we cannot get firewood
And we can't get rain?
Where do they get the animal skins?
Here!
Where do they get the workers to work those machines?
Here!
Where do they get the buyers for those shoes
Here!

The little amount of money they give us,
We give back to them;
The profit on our work,
On our blood,
They take to Europe,
To develop their own countries.
The money they have already sent to Europe
Paid for those machines and buildings a long time ago.
Son of Gathoni, what did I tell you?
A handful of peanuts is thrown to a monkey
When the baby it is holding is about to be stolen!
If all the wealth we create with our hands
Remained in the country,
What would we not have in our village?
Good public schools,
Good houses for the workers,
Good houses for the peasants,
And several other industries
In which the unemployed could be absorbed.
Do you, son of Gathoni, call this a house?
Would you mind living in a more spacious house?
And remember the majority are those
Who are like me and you!
We are without clothes.
We are without shelter.
The power of our hands goes to feed three people:
Imperialists from Europe,
Imperialists from America,
Imperialists from Japan,
And of course their local watchmen.
But son of Gathoni think hard
So that you may see the truth of the saying
That a fool's walking stick supports the clever:
Without workers,
There is no property, there is no wealth.
The labour of our hands is the real wealth of the country.
The blood of the worker

Led by his skill and experience and knowledge
Is the true creator of the wealth of nations.
What does that power, that blood, that skill
Get fortnight after fortnight?
Something for the belly!
Wa Gathoni, just for the belly!
But it's not even enough for the belly!
It's just to bribe the belly into temporary silence!
What about the three whom I mentioned?
Today all the good schools belong
To the children of the rich.
All the big jobs are reserved
For the children of the rich.
Big shops,
Big farms,
Coffee plantations,
Tea plantations,
Wheat fields and ranches,
All belong to the rich.
All the good tarmac roads lead to the homes of the rich.
Good hospitals belong to them,
So that when they get heart attacks and belly ulcers
Their wives can rush them to the hospitals
In Mercedes Benzes.
The rich! The rich!
And we the poor
Have only dispensaries at Tigoni or Kĩambu.
Sometimes, these dispensaries have no drugs,
Sometimes people die on the way,
Or in the queues that last from dawn to dusk . . .

WANGECI:
Oh, well, independence did come!

NJOOKI: [*Sings Gĩtiiro**]
Let me tell you

---

*Gĩtiiro: name of a dance song, a form of opera

For nobody is born wise
So although it has been said that
The antelope hates less he who sees it
Than he who shouts its presence,
I'll sing this once,
For even a loved one can be discussed.
I'll sing this once:
When we fought for freedom
I'd thought that we the poor would milk grade cows.
In the past I used to eat wild spinach.
Today I am eating the same.

GĪCAAMBA: [*Continuing as if he does not want his thoughts to wander away from the subject of foreign-owned companies and industries*]

Yes,
What did this factory bring to our village?
Twenty-five cents a fortnight.
And the profits, to Europe!
What else?
An open drainage that pollutes the air in the whole country!
An open drainage that brings diseases unknown before!
We end up with the foul smell and the diseases
While the foreigners and the local bosses of the company
Live in palaces on green hills, with wide tree-lined avenues,
Where they'll never get a whiff of the smell
Or contract any of the diseases!

KĪGŪŪNDA: [*Sighs and shakes his head in disbelief*]

Oooh!
I have never worked in a factory.
I didn't know that conditions in industries are that bad.

GĪCAAMBA:

To have factories and even big industries
Is good, very good!
It's a means of developing the country.
The question is this: Who owns the industries?
Who benefits from the industries?
Whose children gain from the industries?
Remember also that it's not only the industrial tycoons

Who are like that!
Have you ever seen any tycoon sweating?
Except because of overweight?
All the rich wherever they are . . .
Tajiri wote duniani . . .
Are the same,
One clan!
Their mission in life is exploitation!
Look at yourself.
Look at the women farm labourers,
Or those that pick tea-leaves in the plantations:
How much do they get?
Five or seven shillings a day.
What is the price of a kilo of sugar?
Five shillings!
So with their five shillings:
Are they to buy sugar,
Or vegetables,
Or what?
Or have these women got no mouths and bellies?
Take again the five shillings:
Are they for school fees,
Or what?
Or don't those women have children
Who would like to go to school?
Well, independence did indeed come!

NJOOKI:
You'll have to shut those mouths of yours!
It hates less he who sights it
Than he who shouts its presence.
Was it not only the other day
That the police beat you
When you went on strike
Demanding an increase in wages?
Did you get anything
Apart from broken limbs?
Your rumour-mongering
Will cost you lives.

WANGECI:
>Was it not the same language
>You people used to talk during the rule of the wealthy whites?
>When will you ever be satisfied? You people!
>Dwellers in the land of silence were saved by silence!

KĪGŪŪNDA:
>Dicussions breed ideas.
>And ideas cannot be hauled about like missiles.
>Discussions breed love, Gīkūyū has stated.

GĪCAAMBA *lifts up* KĪGŪŪNDA's *arm. They sing.* GĪCAAMBA *sings solo and then they both join in the chorus. They dance around the stage, the two women looking on.*

GĪCAAMBA:
>*Here at wa Gathoni's place*
>*I will spend night and day*
>*Till I am sent for by post.*

CHORUS:
>*Here at wa Gathoni's place*
>*I will spend night and day*
>*Till I am sent for by post.*

GĪCAAMBA:
>*I'll talk about workers*
>*And also about peasants*
>*For in unity lies our strength.*

CHORUS:
>*I'll talk about workers*
>*And also about peasants*
>*For in unity lies our strength.*

GĪCAAMBA:
>*Foreigners in Kenya*
>*Pack your bags and go*
>*The owners of the homestead have come.*

CHORUS:
>*Foreigners in Kenya*
>*Pack your bags and go*
>*The owners of the homestead have come.*

ALL:
>   I'll defend my fatherland
>   With the sword of revolution
>   As we go to the war of liberation.

ALL:
>   I'll defend my fatherland
>   With the sword of revolution
>   As we go to the war of liberation.

GĪCAAMBA:
>   Poverty! Poverty!
>   Nobody can govern over poverty
>   For poverty is like poison in a body.
>   Exploitation and oppression
>   Have poisoned our land.

A knock at the door: all turn their eyes to the door. AHAB KĪOI WA
KANORU, JEZEBEL, SAMUEL NDUGĪRE *and* HELEN *enter and stand near the
door, so that for a time there are two opposing groups in the house.*
AHAB KĪOI *and* JEZEBEL *are dressed in a way that indicates wealth and
wellbeing. But the* NDUGĪRE *family is dressed in a manner which shows
that they have only recently begun to acquire property.* KĪOI *for
instance is dressed in a very expensive suit with a hat and a folded
umbrella for a walking stick.* JEZEBEL *too has a very expensive suit with
expensive jewellery. But* NDUGĪRE *and* HELEN *have clean, tidy but
simpler clothes. They all take out handkerchiefs with which they keep
wiping their eyes and faces because of the smoke in the house. They
also cough and sneeze rather ostentatiously.* KĪGŪŪNDA *and* WANGECI
are worried because there are not enough seats in the house. GĪCAAMBA
and NJOOKI *look at the visitors with completely fearless eyes. As* KĪOI
*and his group enter moving close to one wall of the house to avoid
contact with the* GĪCAAMBAS, *one of them causes the title-deed to fall to
the ground. They don't pick it up. And because of their worry about
seats and the excitement at the arrival of the* KĪOIS, KĪGŪŪNDA *and his
wife do not seem to have their minds on the fallen title-deed.* GĪCAAMBA
walks to the title-deed and picks it up. All eyes are now on GĪCAAMBA
and they give way to him. GĪCAAMBA *looks at the title-deed, then at the*
KĪOI *group then at the* KĪGŪŪNDA *family. He hangs the title-deed back
on the wall.* GĪCAAMBA *and* NJOOKI *go out.*

KĪGŨŨNDA: [*Relieved*]
Come in, come in
Why are you standing?

As he says that, he is giving them seats. KĪOI *sits on the chair which* KĪGŨŨNDA *had been repairing.* NDŨGĨRE *and his wife sit on the bed, and* KĪOI'*s wife sits on an empty water tin or small water drum. They sit in such a way that the* KĪOI *group is on one side and the* KĪGŨŨNDA *family on the other side, at least they should be seen to be apart, or to be in two opposing camps.* WANGECI *now cleans her hand with a rug or with her upper garment or with her dress, and shakes hands all round. She then removes the pot from the fire and busies herself with plates and engages in other chores connected with the reception of the visitors.*

KĪOI:
We are not staying . . .
You were at our place this morning,
I take it?

KĪGŨŨNDA:
Yes, I am the one who milked the cows
And I even helped the tractor driver to load it.
But it was very early,
You had not yet woken up.
The only other person whom I saw was the Securicor guard
As the company car came to fetch him away.

NDŨGĨRE:
Who is the tractor driver?

KĪOI:
He is an old hand at the farm.
Even when the farm belonged to the white man
We had nicknamed him Kanoru . . .
We gave him the same name as my father . . .
The tractor driver worked there.

KĪGŨŨNDA:
Kanoru's?
I too used to work there
Before I was sent to detention at Manyani.

JEZEBEL: [*To* NDŨGĨRE *but loud enough for everybody to hear*]
That tractor driver is very mature.

He does not argue back.
He does not demand higher wages.
He just believes in hard work,
Praising our Lord all the time.
He is a true brother-in-Christ.

NDUGĪRE:
You have spoken nothing but the truth.
If all people were to be saved,
And accepted Jesus as their personal saviour,
The conflicts you find in the land would all end.
For everybody,
Whether he does or does not have property,
Whether an employee or an employer,
Would be contented
To remain in his place.

WANGECI *scoops out rice on plates and hands a plateful to everyone.*

JEZEBEL: [*Looks at the food as if she is finding fault with the cooking*]
You know, with me, when lunch time is over,
However hungry I might have been,
I am not able to swallow anything!

KĪOI:
I am also the same,
But I could do with a cup of tea.

WANGECI:
I'll make tea for you.
But you can't come into my house
And fail to bite something.

KĪGŪŪNDA *starts to eat heartily.* WANGECI *is busy putting water for tea on
the firestones.*

KĪOI:
Let's say grace.
Sister-in-Christ!
Say grace before we eat.

HELEN: [*Eyeing the* KĪGŪŪNDAS *with ferocious disapproval*]
Let's all pray . . .
God, Creator of Heaven and Earth,
You the owner of all things on earth and in heaven,

We pray you bring to an end
The current wickedness in the land:
Breaking into banks and other people's shops,
Stealing other people's coffee,
Placing obstructions on highways,
All this being Satan's work to bring ruin to your true servants.
Oh, God our Father
Tame the souls of the wicked
With thy sword of peace,
For we your servants are unable to sleep
Because of the terror inflicted on us by the wicked.
You to whom all the things on earth do belong
Show the wicked that everybody's share comes from Heaven,
Be it poverty or riches.
Let us all be contented with our lot.
We ask you to bless this food,
And add unto us that of the Holy Spirit;
We ask you in the name of your only Son,
Jesus Christ, our Lord.

ALL:

Amen.

After the grace, KĪOI *and* JEZEBEL *take a spoonful each and then they are satisfied. But* NDUGĪRE *and* HELEN *eat without any inhibitions.*

KĪOI:

You might perhaps be wondering
Why we have come here today.
Do you know him?
He is our brother-in-Christ.

NDUGĪRE: [*Standing up to give testimony*]

My name is Samuel Ndugīre
I am a man who has received the tender mercy of the Lord,
Since the year 1963.
Before then I used to be a very bad homeguard.
I used to kill people,
And to do many other terrible deeds
As was the habit among the homeguards of those days.
In our village they had baptized me Kĩmeendeeri

Because of the way I used to crush people's heads.
But the Lord called unto me in 1963,
It was the midnight of December twelve,
And he told me:
Ndugīre . . . the only good freedom is that of the soul.
Leave your fishing net behind
Follow me now,
And I shall make you a fisher of men.

The KĪOI *group sings*

I shall make you fishers of men
Fishers of men, fishers of men,
I shall make you fishers of men,
If you follow me
      If you follow me
      If you follow me
I shall make you fishers of men
If you follow me.

Since then my affairs started improving.
I and my sister-in-Christ
Were given a few shops by God.
It's from those shops,
That we now and then get a shilling or two
For clothes for our children,
For school fees,
And for petrol.
And quite recently,
God showed us a tiny garden in the settled area.
It is a tiny garden of about a hundred acres.
But it has a good crop of tea.
The same Lord then took us by the hand,
To inside a bank
Where he enabled us to get a loan with which to buy it.
Now you see I did not take out
Even a cent from my pocket.
And yet I am milking cows,
And I am harvesting tea.
That's why I always praise the Lord
Without any fear.

KĪOI, JEZEBEL, HELEN *and* NDUGĪRE *sing while* KĪGŪŪNDA *and* WANGECI *sit completely amazed.*

> We praise you
> Jesus lamb of God
> Jesus your blood cleanses me
> I praise you Lord.

As they come to the end of the verse they are seized by the spirit. NDUGĪRE *starts another hymn. He claps and the other three join in, dancing about with joy.*

> I step gently on the road
> On my way to heaven.
> I am sure that I'll get there
> To rest for ever with the other saints.

> Thank you Lord my guide
> With Jesus Christ as my bread of life
> And the Holy Spirit as my water of life
> I'll never go hungry or thirsty.

> Wild animals and diseases
> And even poverty can't get at me
> For they are frightened by the bright flames around me
> For I am completely dressed up in the splendour of God.

KĪGŪŪNDA: [*Shouting at them*]
> What do you want?

JEZEBEL *is startled by the sudden unexpected shout and she falls down.* NDUGĪRE *and* HELEN *rush to where she has fallen on the floor. They fuss around her, lift her to her feet and dust off her clothes, all the time casting murderous glances at* KĪGŪŪNDA. WANGECI *is worried and she tries to make the tea. She looks about for the tea-leaves. Then she shouts:*

WANGECI:
> Oh, dear, we have no tea-leaves.
> They were finished last night
> And I forgot to buy more.
> [*Showing them the sugar*]
> I only remembered to buy sugar.

KĪOI:
>   It does not matter . . .
>   Even without having given witness,
>   I would like to say this:
>   The other day the Lord our Master
>   Came to me and to my sister-in-Christ
>   And he told us:
>   How can you light a lamp,
>   And then cover it with a tin?
>   After praying hard and humbling ourselves before him,
>   The Lord our Master told us
>   That we should show people the way
>   To enter the church of God
>   So that we can all praise the Lord together!

KĪGŪŪNDA: [*Slowly, without shouting*]
>   What do you want?

KĪOI:
>   We want you to enter the Church!

JEZEBEL:
>   You and your wi-wi-wi-
>   And Wangeci.

HELEN:
>   Come out of the muddy trough of sins!

NDUGĪRE:
>   Praise the Lord.

KĪOI:
>   To enter the Church is easy.
>   But you must first stop living in sin.

JEZEBEL:
>   You must be baptized.

NDUGĪRE:
>   You do a church wedding.

HELEN: [*Showing her wedding ring*]
>   Give Wangeci a wedding ring.

KĪGŪŪNDA:
>   Sin, did you say?

JEZEBEL:

Yes, you and Wangeci have been living in sin.

WANGECI:

But God has blessed us and given us children.

HELEN:

Children of sin.

KĪGŪŪNDA:

Sins . . . Sins!

KĪOI:

We have brought you the tidings
So that when our Lord comes back
To separate goats from cows
You'll not claim
That you had not been warned.
Repent. Come out of the darkness.

KĪOI
JEZEBEL
HELEN
NDUGĪRE
} : [*Singing*]

When Jesus comes back
To take home his amazing ones,
The amazing ones being the people
Saved by the Lord.
They will shine bright as the star
The great northern star
And the beauty of his amazing ones
Will shine like the stars
And you children, and you children . . .

KĪGŪŪNDA *shouts at them, moving threateningly towards them,*
mimicking them at the same time. In fright, JEZEBEL *drops her bag on*
the floor. She does not pick it up as she and HELEN *flee to near the door.*
Near the door, JEZEBEL *remembers her handbag on the floor and she*
tries to gesture to HELEN *to go back for the handbag. But* HELEN *refuses.*
JEZEBEL *moves stealthily towards the bag, picks it up and runs back to*
where HELEN *is standing. All this time* KĪGŪŪNDA *is giving* KĪOI *and*

NDUGĪRE *a piece of his mind. As he moves towards them, they move* *backwards (eyes to the door) at the same time gesturing to* KĪGŪŪNDA *to be cool and patient.*

KĪGŪŪNDA:
>And you the children!
>The amazing ones!
>Sins! sins!
>*Wapi!*
>This is mine own wife,
>Gathoni's mother,
>I have properly married her
>Having paid all the bridewealth
>According to our national ways.
>And you dare call her a whore!
>That we should now be blessed by a human like me!
>Has he shaken hands with God?
>Let me tell you one thing Mr Kīoi.
>Every home has its own head
>And no outsider should interfere in other people's homes!
>Go away, you devils!

As he says the last words, he rushes for the sword. Seeing him take the sword, the KĪOIS *and the* NDUGĪRES *flee followed by* KĪGŪŪNDA *holding the sword.* KĪGŪŪNDA *comes back, laughing and swinging the sword in a kind of victory dance, mimicking them.*

KĪGŪŪNDA:
>Jesus should hurry up
>And come back for his amazing ones . . .

WANGECI: [*Upset*]
>See what you have now done,
>Chasing away our guests.
>You did not let them say what had really brought them here.
>Tomorrow you'll be without a job!

Before KĪGŪŪNDA *answers, a car hoots. After a second* GATHONI *comes, running. She is dressed in new clothes, new platform shoes and has a new handbag. She has also got new earrings. She now stands as if she is in a fashion parade.*

WANGECI:
>Gathoni, from where did you get these clothes?

GATHONI *removes her handbag from one shoulder to the other, then she walks across the stage haughtily, and she cannot take her eyes from her new self. She walks about as if she is still in a beauty contest or fashion parade.*

GATHONI:
   Oh, this dress?
   John Mūhūūni bought it for me.

WANGECI:
   What about these shoes?

GATHONI:
   Platform shoes! He bought them too.

KĪGŪŪNDA:
   Mūhūūni, son of Kīoi?
   Son of Ahab Kīoi wa Kanoru?

GATHONI:
   Yes!

Another hooting. GATHONI *takes out a lipstick and begins to paint her lips red.*

KĪGŪŪNDA:
   Listen.
   When did Kīoi's son marry you?
   I want you to take back this dress to him!
   And all these other fineries of a whore.

WANGECI:
   Even these shoes worn by rebels!

GATHONI:
   And I go back to my rags?

KĪGŪŪNDA:
   A man brags about his penis however small.
   A poor house, but mine!
   Don't overstep the boundaries, else you get lost.

GATHONI: [*For a second stopping applying lipstick*]
   Who is the girl who does not like being well dressed?
   Who does not like to feel that she is human at times?
   So that when now and then she steps on the road
   People's eyes turn to her,

And gasp, there goes Miss Gathoni.
It's poverty and not riches
That forces a woman to go without perfume.

WANGECI:
Do you see how you answer your father?
Don't you know a maiden once drowned in a sea of sweetness!
And where are you going?

GATHONI:
John Mūhūūni wants me to accompany him to the coast.
Mombasa, for a week.

WANGECI:
Mombasa! Swahililand?
Do you think to be smiled at is to be loved?
You'll now get lost.

KĪGŪŪNDA:
If you go to Mombasa,
Then find another home!

Now the hooting continues. GATHONI *puts things back in her handbag.
For a time it looks as if she is torn between her loyalty to her parents and
her loyalty to John Mūhūūni. When she hears another hooting sound,
she walks to the door, turns once to her parents and says 'Goodbye'.
She goes out.* KĪGŪŪNDA *sits down on a chair and supports his head in
his cupped hands, dejected.* WANGECI *slowly walks to the door and
peers outside. Then she comes back and she too slumps into a seat.
There is silence between them, there is complete silence in the house.
After some time,* WANGECI *begins to nod her head as if a new idea has
occurred to her. She stands up and walks slowly to her husband's side
and puts a hand on his shoulder.*

WANGECI:
Don't be so dejected.
A parent is never nauseated
By the mucus from his child's nose.
A she-goat suckles its young
However deformed.
I have just thought of something,

[*Smiling*]
Couldn't that be the reason?

KĪGŪŪNDA:
The reason what?

WANGECI:
Why the Kīois want you and me
To first have a church wedding?

KĪGŪŪNDA:
Why?

WANGECI:
You have eyes and can't see?
Or has the language of the eyes
Become as hard as the language of the ear?

[WANGECI *walks to the title-deed and takes it off the wall*]
You yourself had earlier thought
That they were visiting us
To talk to you about this, your one acre,
Because of the insecticide factory
They and their foreign friends want to build.
Didn't you even show me the letter from Ikuua wa Nditika?
Kīoi did not say a thing about it.
And if they had come here
On account of your piece of land,
Kīoi would have brought Ikuua along.
Our title-deed is now out of danger!

[WANGECI *returns the title-deed to its original place on the wall*]
So what else would make them want
To see us two in a church wedding?
Think!

KĪGŪŪNDA:
So what?

WANGECI:
Gathoni! Gathoni and John Mūhūūni!
Didn't you also think that they were coming
To tell us that
Our daughter should not keep the company of their son?
Did they mention anything of the sort?

Did they say they don't want Gathoni and John Mūhūūni
together?

KĪGŪŪNDA *raises his head. He and* WANGECI *look at each other. Then*
KĪGŪŪNDA *nods his head several times as if he too has suddenly seen the
light.*

END OF ACT ONE

ACT TWO

Scene One

Inside Kīgūūnda's house. Another day. KĪGŪŪNDA, WANGECI,
GĪCAAMBA *and* NJOOKI *are all seated as if in an intense discussion. They
are eating porridge.* WANGECI *and* NJOOKI *are also shelling maize grains
from maize cobs. They are all wearing working clothes. It's evening.
The sun is setting. In the course of this scene, it progressively gets dark
and* WANGECI *has to light a hurricane lamp.*

GĪCAAMBA:
    . . . Leave these people alone.
    They are just playing about with you,
    In the same way a cat plays about with a mouse,
    Kowing that the mouse will end up in the cat's belly!
KĪGŪŪNDA:
    We are looking at it this way!
    It's obvious that Kîoi does not want his son
    To marry from mere pagans!
GĪCAAMBA: [*Doubtingly*]
    Ahab Kīoi wa Kanoru.
    Is that what he told you?
KĪGŪŪNDA:
    Eh . . . Eh . . . What?
GĪCAAMBA:
    That he wants his son
    To marry Gathoni, your daughter?
WANGECI:
    Not in so many words
    They only hinted at it . . .

GĨCAAMBA:
> Promises do not mean delivery.
> Clouds may be in the sky
> But it does not mean it'll rain!

NJOOKI:
> You people! You people!
> A tooth smiles at a spear.
> The rich never marry from the poor.
> The rich only want to find ways
> Of continuing to drink people's blood.

GĨCAAMBA:
> And how does religion come into it?
> Religion is not the same thing as God.
> All the religions that now sit on us
> Were brought here by the whites.
> Even today the Catholic religion
> Is still called the Roman Catholic Church.
> P.C.E.A. belongs to Scottish protestants.
> The Anglican church belongs to the English.
> The Orthodox belongs to the Greeks.
> The Baptist belongs to the Americans.
> There are many more religions
> Which have been brought here by imperialists from America,
> And which tell us we should give them a tenth of all that we
>   produce.
> Where does the ten per cent go?
> To America.
> Then they send back to us ten shillings
> Taken from the tenth portion we sent them,
> And they tell us:
> This is American aid to your local churches.
> And we give them a standing ovation.
> When the British imperialists came here in 1895,
> All the missionaries of all the churches
> Held the Bible in the left hand,
> And the gun in the right hand.
> The white man wanted us

To be drunk with religion
While he,
In the meantime,
Was mapping and grabbing our land,
And starting factories and businesses
On our sweat.
He drove us from our best lands,
Forcing us to eke a living from plots on road sides
Like beggars in our own land,
Some of us dying in his tea and coffee plantations
Others dying in his factories.
Had we not woken up
And sworn a readiness to die
Fighting against the British imperialists,
Where would Kenya be today?
The white man had arranged it all
To completely soften our hearts
To completely cripple our minds with religion!
And they had the audacity to tell us
That earthly things were useless!

[*Singing*]

    Goats and cows and money
    Are not important.
    What is important
    Is the splendid face of Jesus.

    I glance here
    I glance there
    And I see a huge bonfire
    In Devil's Hell
    And I ask myself:
    What can I do
    To avoid the Hell's fire?

But they, on this earth, this very earth,
They are busy carousing on earthly things, our wealth,
And you the poor are told:

Hold fast unto the rosary,
Enter the church,
Lift up your eyes unto the heavens.

NJOOKI   ⎫
          ⎬ : [*Singing*]
GĨCAAMBA ⎭

Believe in God
And He'll take care of all your problems,
He will show you all the good things
And remove all the evils from you
Through Jesus you'll get your share in heaven.
    Believe in God
    Believe in God
    Believe in God
    And trust in Him.

GĨCAAMBA:
Can't you remember
The days of our freedom struggle?
Was it not the religious leaders
Who used to be sent to us in detention camps
At Manyani
Mageta
Hola
Mackinon Road
Wamũũmũ
To tell us:
Surrender, surrender, confess the oath,
That's what Jesus tells you today!
[*Sadly*]
I remember one man,
Whom we had nicknamed Patriot Son of Njeeri,
Because of his patriotic courage.
He was a brave fighter,
So feared by the enemy
That the enemy soldiers would not go near any place
Rumoured to be wa Njeeri's area of operations.
When he was finally caught,
His gun having jammed,

Wa Njeeri was sentenced to hang.
I remember one priest,
Even today he is still around preaching,
Who used to trail wa Njeeri in the cell:
Repent, repent.
Confess the oath,
Reveal where the others are hiding.
All this as if we were not fighting
For the liberation of our country,
The liberation of our lands and our wealth!
Patriot Son of Njeeri
Just shot saliva into the fellow's priestly mouth
And told him that
He, a patriot, would never betray the other patriots to foreigners
Because of his belly!
He told him with great courage:
I Patriot Son of Njeeri
Will never sell the masses
Or sell my country for money!
I would rather die.

NJOOKI *starts a song and they all join in:*

> *I'll never betray this land,*
> *I'll never allow the greed for money to*
> *   guide me*
> *Like Warūhiū and Luka wa Kahangara.*

GĪCAAMBA:
The same colonial church
Survives even today.
Did the leopard ever change its spots?
A kid steals like its mother.
The chameleon family
Has never changed its backridge.
Wa Gathoni, the war was hard fought!

WANGECI:
The church has changed a lot.
They now beat drums and play guitars in church!

They sometimes use traditional tunes
To fit in religious words!

NJOOKI:

Yes!
But the song is the same song . . .
The word the same word . . .
The aim the same!
And the intentions are still the same!
You!
You don't need to have words rammed down your throat!
You!
The earthly water is bitter!

GĪCAAMBA:

[*Singing*]

And even today the earthly water is still bitter
From homesteads to workplaces,
From the children to grown-ups
The earthly water is bitter, what shall we drink?

ALL: [*Joining in*]

If you go to any office to seek help,
You find the occupant is glum,
If you try to enter inside,
He growls at you, 'I'm busy'
All because the earthly water is bitter.

NJOOKI: [*Continues singing alone to prove that the aim of all these religious hymns is to point the way to heaven*]

Even now, the earthly water is bitter
From homesteads to workplaces,
Drink Jesus and he'll quench your thirst
For the earthly water is bitter.

[*Stops singing but changes to preaching*]

Rest not your souls on this earth.

[*Goes to the wall, takes the title-deed and raises it high*]

Lay not your treasures on this earth.

ALL: [*Singing*]

This world is not my home
I am just a passer-by.

>*All my joys await me in heaven*
>*Where all the saved have gone.*
>*I'll never worry over earthly homes.*

GĪCAAMBA:
>What about their homes of twenty storeys and more?
>Have they burnt them down?
>It's simply that they don't want us
>To think too much about our shanties,
>And ask ourselves, why!

NJOOKI: [*To* KĪGŪŪNDA, *as if preaching to him but still holding high the title-deed*]
>Blessed are they that go thirsty and hungry
>And endure tribulations in their hearts
>For they shall inherit the Kingdom of God!

GĪCAAMBA: [*Now really worked up*]
>The Kīois of this earth
>Where do they rest their souls?

NJOOKI *points at the title-deed as if she is answering* GĪCAAMBA'*s question. She then hangs back the title-deed on the wall, walking as if she has a rich man's big belly. She then walks back to her seat still imitating the walk of a rich man with a big protruding belly.*

GĪCAAMBA:
>Why didn't Kīoi come
>To tell you that he has increased your wages?
>Or to give you a piece of his own lands?
>Yes, for the earthly treasures are not that important!
>Or is it a sin to increase a worker's wages?
>Religion ... religion ...!
>Religion is the alcohol of the soul!
>Religion is the poison of the mind!
>It's not God who has brought about our poverty!
>All of us were born equally naked.
>Wa Gathoni,
>It's not that we don't work hard:
>I drive a machine all the day,
>You pick tea-leaves all the day,
>Our wives cultivate the fields all the day,

And someone says you don't work hard?
The fact is
That the wealth of our land
Has been grabbed by a tiny group
Of the Kīois and the Ndugīres
In partnership with foreigners!
Accompany them to church, if you like!
No one regrets the going as the returning.
Take care you don't lose four
While running after eight.

KĪGŪŪNDA:
Listen.
I am not much after the church.
I don't even go to these haraambes
For stone church buildings
Daily being erected
As if in competition.
But,
And there you have not answered me,
Shall I punish my own daughter and ruin her future
By refusing to have our marriage blessed?

GĪCAAMBA:
There is no marriage which is not blessed.
How else would God have given you Gathoni?
Didn't you pay the bridewealth,
Seeking our people's communal blessings?
Isn't the Ngurario ceremony the true blessings
Of all your family and the nation?
The voice of the people is the voice of God.

NJOOKI:
Marriage is between a man and a woman.
Marriage is a covenant between two people,
Their flesh and soul becoming one
Without money coming into it,
Love pulled by love:
Love the price of love.
Today it's not one human that marries another
But property marrying property,

Money marrying money,
This House marrying that House,
Hearts being taken to the market
And the customers asked:
How many kilos of love do you want?
That's why you find that
Even if modern couples go to church
Or to the District Commissioner,
With the rings and flowers,
They don't spend more than two nights together!
Darling, I'm sorry, but it was not you I loved.
Sugarmummies and sugardaddies
Are now all over the land:
Boys with their mothers,
Girls with their fathers!
What happens to the herd
When the leader has broken legs?

GĪCAAMBA:

They go to church as a fashion.
Some go back to the church only on the day
They are being buried.

WANGECI:

You!
They can't say prayers over your body
Unless you have been baptized
And you have been a churchgoer.

GĪCAAMBA:

Yes, if you are poor.
But if you are a man of property
Or if you have been a leader of this or that
They will pray for you
And sing aloud
How hardworking you used to be.
Haven't you heard it said that
A rich man's fart does not stink?
How many bishops came to the funeral
Of the rich old man who died recently,

And you know very well that
He never even knew the door to any church?
Do you want to say that
If Ikuua wa Nditika died today
His body would not be taken to the altar
By his friends the Kīois?
Don't tell me this and that.
A blessed marriage is when
A human quality is attracted by another human quality.
A blessed marriage is when
Two people accept to be two patriots
Defending their home and nation.

WANGECI:

What's wrong in having a marriage blessed?

NJOOKI:

Were you not told just now?
There's no marriage which is not blessed
Except the one founded on measured love
Or on bank savings!
My wedding for instance was very blessed
Though I didn't take it to their churches.
The Ngurario* ceremony was attended by the whole land.

GĪCAAMBA:

Men, women and children,
The whole community rejoiced together.

KĪGŪŪNDA:

I too was there
And I saw it all!
The women's ululations
Were like trumpets of purest joy . . .

The national Ngurario wedding ceremony of GĪCAAMBA *and* NJOOKI.
Women from the side of the bridegroom enter from one side carrying

---

*Ngurario: the final ceremony in a marriage. Once a couple go through this
ritual, they are supposed to be legally married.

*liquor and other gifts trilling the five ululations for a boy. Women from
the bride's side enter from the other side answering back with the four
ululations for a girl. They meet in the middle and form a circle and the
two sides exchange compliments and gifts through the Gītiiro opera
dance and song.*

AAGACIKŪ [*The bride's clan*]
>Let me give away the hand of Njooki,
>I swore I would never exchange her
>For anybody's property.
>But I'll exchange her for a gourd of honey.
>Give me now the honey
>For which I once took an oath.
>I'll now keep the honey beside the bed
>So every time I wake up I taste a little.
>I, woman of the Njikū clan,
>Have cultivated hills and slopes
>Making sure that Njooki has enough to eat.
>That's why I swore I would never exchange her for property
>That I would only exchange her for honey.
>Huuu! I said I would take her to the home of Gīcaamba Son of
>>Kīhooto
>Where rich honey is kept in skin drums.
>Yes, this is Njooki whom I now take
>Where honey is kept in skin drums,
>Delicacy of many seasons
>A feast in valleys far away.

AAMBŪI [*Women from the bridegroom's clan*]
>Woman with a beautiful gap in the teeth
>I'm still on my way to the Njikū clan
>Looking for Njooki, my bride.
>For I keep on asking myself
>Where will I get the woman
>Who will fill my granary with millet grains?
>I'll come to you, stealthily walking against the walls,
>The same walls against which
>The black goats of the Mbūi clan

Warm themselves and scratch their skins.
Woman of the Njikū clan
I have everything you may now demand of me,
Except that which was stolen from me by the whites.
I have got your honey.
But I'm also hungry though I'll not beg.
Hand me now my Njooki
Through the main entrance into my homestead
And even then, woman of the Njikū clan,
You'll give me my yam with which
To fill the broken gap in my mouth,
For I long ago tightened a belt around my waist
And I swore I would only untie the belt
At Njooki's mother's homestead.

AAGACIKŪ:

Here is the millet gruel, woman of the Mbūi clan,
You who know how to welcome guests!
Now hand me my honey
And my earrings and tobacco
For the beautiful one from the Njikū clan.
As for you the beautiful one from the Mbūi clan,
I have got your yam,
And a crop of ripened bananas.

The AAGACIKŪ *clan trill the four ululations for a girl. The* AAMBŪI *trill the five ululations for a boy.*

AAGACIKŪ:

Now you have seen
We have given away the hand of Njooki
To the Mbūi clan
So famous in war and peace.
Let's now go back to cultivate our fields
While seeking ways of getting back
Lands stolen from us by the whites.

AAMBŪI:

Yes, we join our two hands
To see if we can defeat the enemy
Of this, our land,
Our beautiful land of Mount Kenya.

*When they finish the Gĩtiiro opera sequence they sing and dance yet
another sequence, expressing joy and triumph.*

> Give way
> Give way
> Else you'll be trodden
> By the herds belonging to the Mbũi clan
> Herds with bells around their necks.

*As soon as they finish and exit, children rush onto the stage pulling the
bride, encircling her, singing and dancing.*

> Hail our herds
> Hail our bride
> She'll fetch water for us from the valley
> And should she refuse
> We back-a-bite her

*And as soon as the children exit, men now enter the stage singing and
dancing. They form a big circle.*

> In whose homestead do you raise the dust of vigour?
> In whose homestead do you raise the dust of happiness?
> I holding a gun in the mountains
> For I see the soot here hangs long and loose from the roof
> I holding a gun in the mountains.
> Whose homestead is this?
> Whose homestead is this?
> I holding a gun in the mountains
> So I can roll down like the young of a rhino
> I holding a gun in the mountains.
> Mother ululate for me
> Mother ululate for me
> I holding a gun in the mountains
> For a white woman once raised hue and cry against me
> I holding a gun in the mountains.

*Women ululate. The dancers get off the stage still singing and dancing.
GĨCAAMBA takes over.*

GĨCAAMBA:
> It was soon after this
> That the colonial government
> Forbade people to sing or dance,
> It forbade a gathering of more than five.

But we went on meeting clandestinely.
We the workers in factories and plantations said in one voice:
We reject slave wages!
Do you remember the 1948 general strike?

*A procession of workers with placards bearing political slogans enter.
They shout different slogans: 'We want higher wages; Down with
prices; Up with Uhuru, Down with Imperialism; Down with traitors,
Up with patriots; the factories and the country belong to us.' They then
form a line sitting in twos, ready to take the oath of unity in struggle.
The leader utters a particular resolution and the mass repeats after him.
After each resolution, two people go through the arch of banana leaves
to the other side, where two patriots, a woman and a man, are standing
giving out guns. As soon as they get the guns, they stand in a line
marking time ready for the war of liberation.*

LEADER:
    I speak the truth and swear before God
    And before the people present
    And before the ancestors
    I swear by the oath of the masses
    And by the blood of the Kenyan people.
ALL [*Repeat*]
LEADER:
    I'll never let this soil go with foreigners
    Leaving the people of Kenya wretched!
    If I ever let it go,
    May this, the people's oath, destroy me
    And the blood of the masses turn against me.
ALL: [*Repeat*]
LEADER:
    I'll never aid the missionaries in their preaching
    Or follow them
    Betraying our culture and national traditions.
    If I do so,
    May this, the people's oath, destroy me
    And the blood of the masses turn against me.

ALL: [*Repeat*]

LEADER:

> If I am asked to hide weapons
> I shall obey without questions.
> If I am called upon to serve this organization
> By day or night,
> I'll do so!
> If I fail to do so
> May this, the people's oath, destroy me
> And the blood of the poor turn against me.

ALL: [*Repeat*]

LEADER:

> I'll never make a girl pregnant
> And then leave her without a husband
> If I do so,
> May this, the people's oath, destroy me
> And the blood of the masses turn against me.

ALL: [*Repeat*]

LEADER:

> I'll never never divorce
> If I do so,
> May this, the people's oath, destroy me
> And the blood of the masses turn against me.

ALL: [*Repeat*]

LEADER:

> I'll always help this organization,
> With all my strength and property,
> I'll help members of this organization,
> So that if a bean falls to the ground
> We split it amongst ourselves.

ALL: [*Repeat*]

LEADER:

> Therefore I'll never eat alone
> Forgetting fellow comrades and patriots,
> If I do so,
> May this, the people's oath, destroy me
> And the blood of the masses turn against me.

ALL: [*Repeat*]

When all are in line with weapons, the LEADER *makes them go through military drills, he then inspects a guard of honour (or the other way round), and then they march out singing joyfully and defiantly.*

> *We were happy as we went to battle*
> *We were happy as we returned victorious*
> *Our spirits were high*
> *As we went and returned.*

> *When we got to Rūirū River*
> *We found it in floods*
> *Warūingī ordered us to make a bridge*
> *Death in struggle is welcome.*

> *A little further on*
> *We came across a traitor,*
> *Who threatened to shout our presence,*
> *Waruingī said, let him shout*
> *And a bullet will shout him down.*

GĪCAAMBA:
> It was soon after this that
> I too fled into the mountains
> To join the people's guerrilla army
> Here in Limuru
> We were led by Warūingī and other patriots.

A battle between Mau Mau guerrillas and British soldiers with their African homeguards breaks out. The Mau Mau guerrillas are victorious, killing a few enemy soldiers, capturing some of their weapons and clothes, capturing one or two enemy soldiers, and making the others run away. The Mau Mau patriots now march on the stage singing victory songs.

> When our Kīmaathi ascended the mountains
> He asked for strength and courage
> To defeat the imperialist enemy.

After marching, they go out, still singing.

ĪCAAMBA:
    We were not given freedom
    We bought it with our blood,
    We the peasants, workers and children.
    Wa Gathoni,
    Do you want to say that
    That blood was not blessed?
    If we had agreed with those
    Who used to tell us,
    Get saved, surrender,
    Think of your life only and
    You'll go to heaven,
    Kenya would still be under colonial rule.
    Blessings! Blessings!
    Blessings are born of patriotic unity!
    Blessings come to a people,
    When they love their country
    And they unite to produce wealth,
    Uniting in toil
    And in sharing out without greed,
    And without discrimination between sexes!
    Blessings come to a people
    When they reach a stage where
    If a bean falls to the ground
    They split it among themselves.
    Blessings will come to us
    When we struggle and fight for our rights
    And defend Kenya against internal and foreign exploitation.
ʷANGECI [*Standing up and speaking bitterly*]
    I don't much care
    If Gathoni marries into the Kĩoi family or not.
    All I care is for Gathoni to marry a man
    Who will look after her.
    Whether she marries into a rich man's home
    Like that of Kĩoi's business partner,
    Ikuua wa Nditika,
    Even though he never goes to church,

Or she marries one of your sons, Gīcaamba,
All I want is for her
To live well.

WANGECI *starts collecting things together and lighting up the lamp in a way that shows that the* GĪCAAMBAS *are no longer welcome*

NJOOKI   [*Getting the hint and turning to* GĪCAAMBA]
You have talked too much
A priest without a collar!

GĪCAAMBA:
I am a priest of peace
And patriotic unity.

NJOOKI:
Why then don't you go to a seminary!
Let's go home now
For tomorrow is back to work.

GĪCAAMBA:
Give us leave to go.
But think about what I've said.
For although Gīkūyū once said
That nobody ever repents another man's sins
Yet a leader who never listens
Is not a leader at all.

NJOOKI *and* GĪCAAMBA *leave.* KĪGŪŪNDA *remains seated but deep in thought. But* WANGECI *goes on with her activities still angry.*

KĪGŪŪNDA:
The spear of Gīcaamba's words
Has truly pierced my heart.

WANGECI   [*Angrily*]
Go ahead and let your daughter suffer
All because of the words of a political agitator.
Since when did a person
Try to build his hut
Exactly like that of his neighbour?

KĪGŪŪNDA:
Gīcaamba is an honest man.
He has never turned his back against the people.
He has never betrayed the Mau Mau oaths.

WANGECI:
It's all alright.
You join Gīcaamba in his drunkenness.
You listen to him and get lost.
You!
The burdens of the masses
Are tied with a cord easy to cut
Or carried in a basket full of holes.
Remember when we received Uhuru!
Some people roamed the whole land
Telling us that we should not buy land
For which we had all shed blood!
Wasn't Ikuua wa Nditika one of those agitators
And he had been in detention at Mageta?
Those who had the money
And those who joined hands with homeguards
Or those that got loans
And did not listen to foolish words,
Weren't they the ones
Who bought all the best lands?
We who listened to foolish words,
Where are we now?
Just this verandah for a house.
[*She goes to the wall and pulls off the title-deed*]
And this piece of waste land,
One and a half acres only.
And even then Ikuua wa Nditika
Is still after it!
Let me tell you.
The coward went home safely to tell the tale
And left the brave lying for ever safe on the battlefield!
Gathoni's father,
Let us go to Kīoi's place early tomorrow morning.
Let's go and tell him that we agree with his plans.
His words are good.
His ways are straight.
His style of life is proper.

His church is holy.
His church shows us the only way to life and happiness.
Gīcaamba's words arise out of envy.
Do you hear,
Or am I talking to the deaf?

KĪGŪŪNDA [*He is still deep in thought. He stands and in confusion and agitation walks about the stage. Then he goes and stands near* WANGECI]

We shall not wait for tomorrow morning.
Let's go there this very minute.
Hand me my sword
For a man does not go in the dark with empty hands.

WANGECI *puts the title-deed on the seat. She goes to get the sword.*
KĪGŪŪNDA *puts on his coat. Then he takes the sword from* WANGECI *and hides it under the coat.* WANGECI *also puts on her coat. Then* KĪGŪŪNDA *sees the title-deed on the seat. He picks it up. He looks at it. Then he slowly walks to the wall and hangs it back,* WANGECI *looking on.*
KĪGŪŪNDA *then turns to* WANGECI :
KĪGŪŪNDA:

Let's not go there now, in the dark, for it is very late.
Let's go there tomorrow early in the evening!
Come to think of it,
We do not even have the money
For the wedding ceremony.

END OF SCENE ONE

Scene Two

Kīoi's home, in the evening. A big well-furnished house. Sofa seats, TV, radiogram, plastic flowers on the table, and so on. Electric lights. On the walls are several photographs. On one wall can be seen a board with the words: 'CHRIST IS THE HEAD OF THIS HOUSE, THE UNSEEN GUEST AT EVERY MEAL, THE SILENT LISTENER TO EVERY CONVERSATION'. *There is also a picture of a hairy Nebuchadnezzar turned into an animal.* JEZEBEL, NDUGĪRE *and* HELEN *are at table. The table has all sorts of dishes. There is also water on the table in a huge glass container. A*

WAITER *stands by.* IKUUA WA NDITIKA, *a man with a belly as huge as that of a woman about to deliver, is seated away from the dining table and is busy collecting his things, bits of paper and so on into a small suitcase.* KĨOI *is standing near him waiting for* IKUUA *to go so he can join the others at table. As soon as* IKUUA *finishes collecting his things, he stands up and makes as if to move.*

JEZEBEL:

Are you sure you won't take a bite?
A cup of tea even,
And it is easy to get it ready.

IKUUA:

I prefer a beer
Or a glass of wine,
But I know that you are all saved, Jesus-is-my-Saviour.
[*They all laugh*]
Anyway you know very well that
When I am not in a hurry
I do take your meals.
I left my Range Rover way down at the gate
And the driver might fall asleep.
Besides, his home is very far from my place
And on driving me home he has to walk back all that way.
Let me go.

[*He makes as if to move and then he turns to* KĨOI. *They walk a step or two and talk as if in a private conference but loud enough for the others to hear*]

Listen Mr Kĩoi.
Don't forget that business about the insecticide factory.
Our foreign friends want to start as soon as possible.
As you know,
The main problem with such a factory
Is that it's bound to produce a lot of smelly gases
And therefore it cannot be built in an area
Where important people live.
What we need is a place like Kĩgũũnda's
Or any other place similarly situated.

       The poor are many in Kenya.
[*They laugh*]
       Their laziness is what is driving them
       To sell their strips of land.
       But if you don't want your name as one of the local directors to
          appear,
       We can use your wife's name
       Or that of John Mūhūūni, your son.
       That's what most people are doing these days,
       Because of income tax,
       And also to cover up a little,
       For poverty has no governor.
       It's better to sometimes cover up our eating habits
       Rather than show the poor our mastications!
       Being a local director of foreign firms
       Is not a very taxing job;
       What they want is just an African's name.
       All we are required to do
       Is to be their watchmen.
       Yes, we could be called their watchdogs!
[*They laugh*]
       Yes, watchdogs for foreign interests!
JEZEBEL:
       Your words Mr Ikuua are very unbecoming,
       They might send you into the everlasting fire.
       You have even refused to renew your marriage in church!
       All you would have been required to do
       Is to throw away one wife.
       It does not matter if the knife falls on the eldest
       And you are left with the youngest
       Provided you go through a proper church ceremony!
IKUUA [*Laughing*]
       I am contemplating marrying a third!
       Mr Kīoi think about the matter,
       But anyway I am coming back soon
       So we can go over the accounts again.
[*Goes out.* KĪOI *joins the others at table*]

HELEN:
> That man has become really wealthy.

JEZEBEL:
> Oh, he is wealth itself!

NDUGĪRE [*Trying to change the subject*]
> So your son John Mūhūūni
> Has not yet returned?

KĪOI:
> From Mombasa? No.
> I had also sent him to Malindi,
> To check on a plot I bought near Watamu Bay!

HELEN:
> What for, so far away?

KĪOI:
> I just want to erect a small hotel!
> About three storeys or so.
> That's why in fact I'm dragging my feet
> Over this business of an insecticide factory.
> At Mombasa and Malindi
> Hotels are very profitable.
> Profits from hotels are more than
> You can get from factories
> Or even from smuggling in coffee or gold or ivory,
> All because of our visitors from abroad!
> What do you call them? Watalii.
> Yes, tourists from America, England, France and Germany.

HELEN:
> Are those the ones I normally see in buses
> Passing by Kīneeniī on the way to the Rift Valley,
> Sometimes stopping by the roadside
> To buy fruit and sheepskins?

NDUGĪRE:
> Tourists?
> I have heard on the radio,
> That there is not a single government ministry
> Which brings as much money into the country
> As the Ministry of Tourism.

I have heard it said
That a man blessed by the Lord
With the ability to provide tourists with all sorts of earthly
    pleasures
Can get lots of money.
Although I believe in self-reliance,
I am also convinced that
Partnership with foreigners can bring quick wealth.

KĪOI:
True,
But these workers cannot let you accumulate!
Every day: I want an increment.
Workers are like the ogres said to have two insatiable mouths.
When they are not demanding a rise in wages
They are asking you for an advance.
My mother is in hospital!
My child has been expelled from school,
Because I have not yet paid his school fees!
My wife has just delivered!

JEZEBEL:
And you know
They won't hear of going to family planning clinics!

KĪOI:
And when a worker decides to go
He does not even give you any notice!

NDUGĪRE:
Do you know what I do with them?
I give them this month's salary
In the middle of the next month.
If you do that,
A worker will never leave you
Unless you sack him.
Of course there are one or two who complain!

JEZEBEL:
This business of not being satisfied,
And of not being contented with one's station in life
As clearly ordained by God,

Comes from not being a good Christian.

HELEN:

These are earthly trials.
We should pray for these people,
Knowing at the same time that
There are many sects
Now misleading the masses.

NDUGĪRE:

Like the sect that calls itself
The church of the poor?
They make us all lose sleep
By their endless night drumming
Shouting: 'Crush Satan!'
Don't they know that Satan is not visible?

JEZEBEL:

I don't blame them.
Many of them cannot read or write,
They don't know A or B or C.

KĪOI:

And even some of these Kikuyu independent churches
which are being revived
Are rather dangerous.
[*Whispering*]
Don't you remember that
Mau Mau oaths used to be taken
Under the cover of those churches?

NDUGĪRE [*Fearfully*]

Is Kīgūūnda one of those people?
Is he a Mau Mau type?
I have never liked that man's eyes.
Do you recall the night he took out his sword against us?

KĪOI:

No, no, Kīgūūnda is not that type at all.
The other workers fear and respect him.
That's why I think that should he be saved
He would lead the other workers into the church.
Some of those workers who waste their energy in beer-halls

Would give up the habit altogether.
Besides, Kīgūūnda is a hard worker
And that's why although he raised a sword against us
I did not dismiss him.

JEZEBEL:

You?
Don't you remember those Mau Mau days?
Wasn't it the servant, supposed to be faithful,
Who used to spy on and betray his European employer?

Dogs bark fiercely. There is a knock at the door. They all look to the door with terrified faces. No one wants to open the door. KĪOI *turns to the* WAITER.

KĪOI:

Go . . . and . . . and . . . open the door.

The SERVANT/WAITER *is also a little scared. He gingerly walks to the door and opens it. A* SECURICOR WATCHMAN *enters and speaks in Kiswahili.*

WATCHMAN:

Sir!
Madam!
There is a man and woman here
And they say they want to see you.
Shall I let them enter?

KĪOI:

Tell them to enter.

Enter KĪGŪŪNDA *and* WANGECI. KĪOI *and his friends are relieved. They literally sigh with relief.*

ALL:

So it was you?

KĪGŪŪNDA ⎫
              ⎬ : Good evening?
WANGECI   ⎭

The WATCHMAN *goes out.*

THE OTHERS:

Good evening.

KĪOI:

We are at table.
Take seats over there.

KĪGŪŪNDA:

We have come because . . .

KĪOI:

Let's first eat,

We are going to talk after.

The WAITER *brings tea and passes near where* KĪGŪŪNDA *and* WANGECI *are sitting. As the* WAITER *passes by,* WANGECI, *thinking that the tea is meant for them, stretches her hand out to pick up one cup. The* WAITER *quickly moves the tray away leaving* WANGECI'*s hand hanging in the air empty.* WANGECI *is very humiliated.*

JEZEBEL:

Please excuse us!

I am afraid we had cooked just enough

For invited guests.

WANGECI [*Trying to cover up her humiliation*]

It does not matter.

We have just eaten,

A supper of a mixture of beans and maize.

HELEN *turns up her nose as if she can smell the foul smell of bean and maize*

KĪGŪŪNDA:

Our only problem is water.

The water around has dried up.

Now our women have to walk for miles.

Wangeci has today been roaming all over

Looking for water,

And even then she could not get any.

Give me a little water

To push down the meal of maize and beans.

JEZEBEL [*To the* WAITER]

Go and fetch water from the drum outside,

You know the one near the pig-sty.

WAITER *hurries out*

NDUGĪRE:

Oh, without water life is such misery!

[*He deliberately takes a glass and fills it with water from the huge jar on the table and empties the glass*]

Before I eat an egg in the morning
I have first to drink a full glass of water.
Some people don't realize that
Water is very vital to the body.
Water is better than tea or even milk.

HELEN:

A well-cared-for body is only possible with water.

The WAITER *brings water, in a cup, and gives it to* KĪGŪŪNDA *who drinks it.*

JEZEBEL:

Yes, because without water,
You cannot clean the body.

KĪOI:

That's why Jesus told the woman from Syria,
I am the water of . . .

NDUGĪRE:

Life!

The others sing: the KĪGŪŪNDAS *watch*
        Thirst and hunger for earthly things
        Is the sleep and death of life.
        Cry unto God your Lord
        And he will save you.
            Life, life,
            The everlasting life
            And you'll never get thirsty.

JEZEBEL:

Let's now say a prayer
To thank God for the food
We have just eaten.

[*She looks at the* KĪGŪŪNDAS]

We thank you Lord our God
For the food you have given us.
Now we humbly lower our eyes
Before your holy presence, Oh Jehovah,
You who are the head of this house
You the unseen guest at every meal
You the silent listener

To every conversation.
We do not want to be like Nebuchadnezzar
Who was turned into a beast
For forgetting to thank you.
That's why we now humbly beg you
To give us spiritual food
And to give us the water of life
So that we shall never never get thirsty.

ALL:

Amen.

The KĪOIS *and the* NDUGĪRES *now leave the table and take more comfortable seats facing the* KĪGŪŪNDAS. *The* SERVANT/WAITER *begins to clear the table.*

KĪOI:

What do you want?

KĪGŪŪNDA [*Clearing his throat*]

We have come because of that matter.

WANGECI:

We have thought a great deal about the matter,
And we came to the conclusion that
We should not put obstacles
To your larger purposes.

KĪOI:

If you have agreed to our plans
We shall now become true friends,
Your house and mine becoming one
In the name of the Lord.

ALL: [*They sing clapping joyfully.* KĪGŪŪNDA *and* WANGECI *join in the singing but they obviously don't know the tune and they often clap out of step*]

Good news
About our Saviour
Has come to us
This is good news.

Yes good news has come
Telling us all

How He forgives
And how he loves us.

Great love is this
Of Christ the helper;
He came down from heaven
Because he felt pity over us.

His name will be sung
From place to place
And all the nations
Will give up their wickedness.

KĪGŪŪNDA:
But there's a small problem!
A modern church wedding
Requires a lot of things.
We cannot enter the holy church
The way we are
With muddy feet
And these rags ever on our shoulders.

JEZEBEL:
You don't need a great deal.
You only need the following:
First is the fee for the officiating priest.
And then robes for the bride.

NDUGĪRE:
And a suit for the bridegroom.

HELEN:
And clothes for bridesmaids and best man.

JEZEBEL:
And for the children,
Who will hold the train!
Then you'll have to set aside a little sum of money
For bread, milk, butter, jam,
And of course for the wedding cake.

HELEN:
Oh, yes, the cake!
The cake is central to a Christian wedding!

NDUGĪRE:

> The Christian Ngurario.
> [*Laughs at the comparison*]

JEZEBEL:

> You!
> Ikuua seems to have taught you unbecoming language!

HELEN:

> What about rings and flowers?

JEZEBEL:

> Oh, yes, I was forgetting those.

KĪOI:

> And you can buy all those
> From my supermarket at Wabera Street.

WANGECI:

> Where shall we get the money for all that?

KĪOI:

> Kĩgũũnda earns a lot of money.
> Don't you deposit some of it
> In a Post Office savings account?

NDUGĪRE:

> You know that we black people
> Have never really mastered the word, savings.
> Yes, setting aside something
> For a rainy day.

KĨGŨŨNDA:

> What do I get a month?
> Two hundred shillings,
> And you call that a lot of money?
> Two hundred shillings a month
> With which to buy clothes, food, water,
> And you know very well
> That prices are daily climbing up!
> A person earning two hundred shillings,
> Can he really cope with the rising prices?

NDUGĪRE: [*Cutting him short*]

> But do you think it possible to have two price categories,
> For those with property
> And those without?

Does God's rain fall on a rich man's fields
Bypassing a poor man's field?

KĪOI:

Not only that my brother-in-Christ.
I give all the workers a hundred or a hundred and fifty!
You, Kĩgũũnda and the tractor driver
Are the only workers who get two hundred shillings.

JEZEBEL: [*As if cracking a joke*]

The tractor driver is very well behaved
And not like you, father of Gathoni.
He never complains about anything.
He never complains about his wages!

KĨGŨŨNDA:

I didn't come here to ask for an increment
Although I won't mind a rise in wages
It's only that the wedding ceremony will cost a lot of money.

KĪOI:

Kĩgũũnda, you are a very wealthy man,
Only that you don't care to know:
You have a lot of land, one and a half acres.
You have a full-time job.
How many thousands who in Kenya today
Cannot boast about a space large enough for a grave even?

NDUGĨRE:

A grave is not even the best comparison
Since there are many state-owned graveyards.
But how many hundreds of Kenyans
Are now roaming all over the country
Looking for any type of job whatever the pay
And they can't get any?

KĨGŨŨNDA:

I wanted to find out
If you could lend us money
To meet the cost of the wedding ceremony.

NDUGĨRE, KĪOI, HELEN *and* JEZEBEL *stare at one another in obvious dismay.* KĪOI *is rapt in thought.*

KĪOI:

That's an easy matter.

I like you.
The other day I even visited you in your home.
But remember what God told Adam and Eve:
There are no free things!
Hakuna cha bure!
No more manna from heaven.

[*Turning to* NDUGĪRE]

If anyone wants free things
He should go to Tanzania
Or to China.

NDUGĪRE:

I have heard it said that
In China there's no private property,
That everything, including women, is shared out.

JEZEBEL ⎫
HELEN   ⎬ : What! Women shared out!

NDUGĪRE:

Yes, they say that in China there's no rich or poor.
But how can a country progress
Unless led by the rich?

KĪOI:

In China, they don't even believe in God.

JEZEBEL:

Didn't the missionaries get there?
Does it mean that all the Chinese,
The whole country, will burn in hell?

KĪOI:

Yes, eight hundred million souls.
To burn for ever!

NDUGĪRE:

Nebuchadnezzar's clansmen.
Let them burn.

HELEN:

Flames jumping in the sky.

NDUGĪRE:

Like flames from a pile of dry firewood.

JEZEBEL:

Their bones breaking: crack! crack!

KĨOI:
> And all because of
> Getting rid of the rich.

KĨGŨŨNDA:
> Does it mean that in China
> People do not now have food, clothes and shelter?

NDUGĨRE:
> Who knows!

KĨOI:
> Just imagine!
> All the people . . .
> If all the people are to become equal like these teeth
> Who would do the work?
> Anyway we in Kenya are very lucky,
> Because we are a Christian nation.
> We worship at the feet of the Lord,
> The same Lord who commanded us all
> To forever sweat over whatever we eat or drink.
> Mr Kĩgũũnda your words are good
> And I am willing to help you.

KĨGŨŨNDA:
> Thank you! Thank you!

KĨOI:
> There are two alternatives.
> You have got one and a half acres of land.
> There is an American-, German- and Japanese-owned company
> Which wants to build an insecticide factory.
> I think Mr Ikuua has already written to you about it!
> If you sell that piece of land,
> You'll get a lot of money.
> With some of that money,
> You can buy land in the Rift Valley
> Or in Maasailand
> And the rest you can bank.

KĨGŨŨNDA:
> I will never sell the piece of land.
> I just wanted . . .

KĨOI:
> I have not finished. I told you there were two alternatives.

You have rejected the first.
The other alternative is to borrow money from a bank
With your one and half acres as security.

KĪGŪŪNDA
WANGECI } : What! Our title-deed to go to a bank!

KĪOI:

Yes, because no bank will lend you money
Without some security.
In fact borrowing from a bank is better
Than borrowing from an individual like me,
Because the bank only requires you
To pay back a little each month.
Now this is how I'm going to help you:
First I'll myself take you to the bank
Of which I am a director
And I will vouch for your integrity.
I'll pledge to withhold from your wages
Whatever the monthly amount
You and the bank will agree.

HELEN:

You, our brother-in-Christ, are very kind-hearted.
Praise the Lord.
[*Turning to* KĪGŪŪNDA]
Do you know that not many people today
Would agree to become a surety
In order that a mere worker might get a bank loan?

NDUGĪRE:

Yes, because a propertied man like Kĩoi
Naturally fears that such a worker
Might fall ill or even die suddenly.

WANGECI:

Anybody can die.
Even millionaires do die.

NDUGĪRE:

Yes, but you will agree that the
Death rate is worse among the poor!

KĪOI:

Mr Kĩgũũnda, what do you have to say?

KĨGŨŨNDA:
>Whether I borrow from you or from a bank
>It is all the same to us.
>I didn't come here to beg.
>But you people are the bankers
>Of what we the poor produce!
>Tomorrow I shall bring the title-deed;
>You and I will take it to the bank.

END OF ACT TWO

ACT THREE

==

Scene One

Kīgūünda's home. The interior is very different from what it was in previous scenes. A new dining table with chairs. On the table is a big suitcase, also new. New plates, cups, basins and so on. A suit hangs on the wall where Kīgūünda's old coat used to hang. On one wall hangs the picture of Nebuchadnezzar exactly like the one in Kīoi's home. On another wall, exactly on the spot where the title-deed used to be, now hangs a board with the inscription: 'Christ is the head . . . etc', again like the one in Kīoi's house. The title-deed is not now anywhere in the house.

The scene opens with KĪGŪÜNDA *and* WANGECI *busy bringing in new things into the house, such as sofa seats, a big standing mirror, a radio and so on.* WANGECI *and* KĪGŪÜNDA *are full of joy at the sight of each item. They are very happy, particularly because their house now looks like the Kīois'.* KĪGŪÜNDA *goes to the board with the inscription 'Christ is the head', takes it off and studies it before putting it back on the wall.* WANGECI *in turn goes to it, dusts it, and then looks at it as if she is studying each letter.* KĪGŪÜNDA *goes to the radio and turns the knobs until he gets a song. He tries to dance to the tune. He then goes to the mirror where he tries on his wedding suit, in the process discarding his old rags and tyre sandals.* WANGECI *goes to the radio, tries the knobs this way and that way, occasionally standing back to admire it or walking about with it or swinging it. She turns to* KĪGŪÜNDA.

WANGECI:
    Why did you buy this?

KĪGŪŪNDA: [*Turning round*]
> Didn't I tell you to try on your clothes?

WANGECI:
> I was admiring you.

WANGECI *goes to the suitcase. She opens it. She starts undressing, getting rid of her old rags. She seems fascinated with the different items of clothing, lifting each in turn, as if she cannot make up her mind where to start. She takes out a huge brassière.*

WANGECI:
> How does one put on this?

KĪGŪŪNDA:
> Why don't you simply wear it as pants?

WANGECI:
> I'll try it on, on the wedding day.

[WANGECI *puts on her wedding robes*]

KĪGŪŪNDA: [*Dusting himself up and admiring himself in his new suit*]
> On that day
> I'll wake very early,
> And put on this suit!

[*Turning round, he is completely mesmerized by* WANGECI *in her white wedding dress*]
> You have turned into a teenager!
> Do you know what this white wedding dress means?
> Its whiteness means that
> You have never known any man.

[*Laughs*]
> On that day
> I shall ask Jishinde Ushinde Studio
> To take a colour picture of you.
> We shall send one picture to the papers
> Taifa Leo. The wedding column.
> I hear that the paper belongs to the Aga Khan
> And they send him a copy of the paper in Europe!
> Imagine!
> Your picture and mine going to the Aga Khan in Europe!
> On that day you and I will walk down the holy aisle
> Holding hands.

[*He tries to hold* WANGECI'S *hand*]
WANGECI:
　　No, it's the bridegroom who enters first.
　　The bride follows, led by her father.
KĪGŪŪNDA:
　　O.K. O.K.!
[*He goes to the radio and stops the music*]
　　I'll then walk ahead with the best man.
[*He walks ahead and then turns his head to see if* WANGECI *is following*]
　　Aren't you following behind me?
WANGECI:
　　I'm coming.
They start walking as if they are really in a church on the wedding day.
A church choir accompanies their mimed enactment of the wedding
ceremony.

　　　　The good news of life
　　　　Is all about Christ the Lord.
　　　　He is our strength.
　　　　He will guide us.
　　　　And should any evil
　　　　Come near us
　　　　Christ is able
　　　　To defend us from evil.
　　　　And when our days on earth are over
　　　　We shall dwell with Jesus
　　　　For ever and ever.

Now WANGECI *and* KĪGŪŪNDA *are standing before an invisible priest.*
They then kneel down before 'him'. The voice of the invisible priest is
heard raised in prayer:
VOICE:
　　Oh, God, our Lord
　　We lower our eyes before you today
　　Asking you to bless this bride
　　And this bridegroom.
　　For you were the one who wrote in the holy book.
　　Thus shall a man leave his father and mother
　　And be joined to his wife

And the two shall become one.
That's why, oh Jehovah, we humbly ask you
To bless this ceremony.
For you also said:
Two people are better than one
For they can see the fruits
Of their labour.
And should one person fall
The other can raise him.
But cursed is the man who falls
And he has no one to raise him.
And if two people should sleep together,
They can warm one another,
But if one sleeps alone,
How can he warm himself?
That's why you Christ the Lord
Went to the holy wedding at Galilee
And you turned water into wine,
The wine which was your blood.
Bless this house of
Winston Smith Kīgũũnda and Rosemary Magdalene Wangeci.
Double the fruits of the labour of their hands.
We ask you all this
In the name of Jesus Christ
Our Lord, Amen.

The prayer is followed by a hymn sung by an invisible church choir:
> God blessed
> The very first wedding
> Of Adam and Eve.
> Even today he still blesses
> Holy matrimony
> When Christians
> Are marrying.
> And afterwards
> When Jesus comes back,
> They'll ascend with him to heaven
> The bride and bridegroom of the Lord.

As the hymn is being sung KĪGŪŪNDA *takes out an invisible ring and puts it on* WANGECI's *finger.* WANGECI *does the same.* KĪGŪŪNDA *now lifts the veil from* WANGECI's *face and kisses her. They kneel down, holding hands. The invisible choir now takes up another hymn.*

> Jesus I have now put on my cross
> To marry my Lord
> Even though
> Others may leave him.
> And you my friend hurry up
> And put on robes of faith
> So that you'll ascend to heaven
> To dwell in God's eternal happiness.

While the hymn is going on KĪGŪŪNDA *and* WANGECI *rise and slowly walk to the reception. They sit, waiting for speeches and gifts.*

KĪGŪŪNDA:
> Speeches bore me.

WANGECI:
> Me, too.
> The man who is now talking
> Never misses a single wedding.

KĪGŪŪNDA:
> And he makes the same speech
> In all the wedding receptions.

WANGECI:
> Look at that one
> Who has just stood to speak.
> He advises couples to do
> What he himself never practises.

KĪGŪŪNDA:
> Yes, he is always beating his wife.

WANGECI:
> Oh, dear,
> That one again!
> She never says anything
> Apart from how beautiful her own wedding was.
> And she ends up crying.
> See.

There she goes.
She has started.
She is weeping . . .

KĪGŪŪNDA:

When will they start bringing us gifts?
Today I want to know
Who our true friends are!
I wonder what the Kîois and the Ndugîres
Will bring us?
Some people can play nasty tricks;
They'll hand you a closed envelope,
But on opening it
You will find they have enclosed only five shillings!
Wait a minute.
That one has stood up.
He will now read the whole Bible
From cover to cover,
And then he will preach
Until tomorrow . . .

WANGECI:

Oh, dear, before we have cut the cake?
Cutting a wedding cake
Which is as white as snow
Or as white as this wedding dress
Is a most wonderful thing.
A wedding without a cake
Is not a Christian wedding at all!

KĪGŪŪNDA:

The speeches are now over.
Let's stand up to cut the cake.
It's a cake, five storeys high!

*They stand up holding an invisible knife. They start cutting the cake.
The choir sings another hymn. They give each other a piece of cake.
They continue cutting it. Suddenly the hymn stops. A car hoots rudely.
But* KĪGŪŪNDA *and* WANGECI *do not hear it. They are totally absorbed in
the ceremony of cutting the cake. Another rude hooting and a car
moves away.* GATHONI *comes in. She is at first taken aback by the*

changes in the house and by the strange behaviour of her parents. She then slumps into a seat and starts weeping. Without realizing that they are still holding each other's hands, her parents stare at GATHONI.

KĪGŪŪNDA ⎫ : What's the matter?
WANGECI ⎭ Where's John Mūhūūni?

GATHONI *goes on weeping.* WANGECI *lets go* KĪGŪŪNDA's *hand and goes to where* GATHONI *is sitting.*

WANGECI:
     What's the matter, my daughter?

GATHONI:
     He . . . he . . . he has jilted me.

WANGECI:
     Who?

GATHONI:
     Jo . . . John . . . Mūhūūni . . .

KĪGŪŪNDA:
     To be jilted is nothing.
     There are many more eligible men in the world.

WANGECI:
     Stop weeping.

GATHONI:
     It . . . is . . . not . . . just . . . that . . .

WANGECI:
     What else?
     Speak. Quickly.

GATHONI:
     We went to Mombasa.
     When we came back to Nairobi
     I told him that
     I was pregnant.

KĪGŪŪNDA ⎫ : Pregnant?
WANGECI ⎭

GATHONI:
     He used to tell me that
     He wanted us to have a baby
     That he would never marry a girl
     Who had not conceived

In case he married someone barren.
At Nairobi, he did not say anything.
But when we reached the village
He suddenly shouted at me
And ordered me to get out of his car,
That he was not responsible for the pregnancy
And that he would never marry a prostitute.

KĪGŪŪNDA:

Do you now see the fruits of your obstinacy?
Did I not forbid you
To go to Mombasa?

WANGECI:

Leave her alone.
Let's go to Kīoi's place now.
He is a good old man,
A Christian,
A man of the church,
A man of integrity,
A man who likes to help others.
He is not the sort who would endure
To see a child like this suffer.
Didn't he tell you that
He wanted your house and his to become one?
Let's go there now,
Even though it is dark,
And tell him.
Let the children marry first.

KĪGŪŪNDA *collects his old rags, about to change. Then he takes the sword. He shouts at Wangeci, 'Change into your old clothes!'*

END OF SCENE ONE

Scene Two

Kīoi's home. KĪOI *and* IKUUA *are alone in the sitting room. They are busy counting money and cheques. Their words can be heard: 'This*

*million and a half comes from the sale of tusks and of lion and leopard
skins to Japan. And these two million come from the maize and salt we
sent to Uganda . . . And these eight millions come from Chepkumbe
coffee . . . ' etc.* IKUUA *is doing most of the talking, while* KĪOI *is merely
grunting assent, and receiving some of the heaps of notes and cheques,
and writing down the figures. As soon as they have finished counting,*
IKUUA *tells* KĪOI: *'It's now your turn to take all this to the bank
tomorrow. And beware of robbers.'* IKUUA *stands up:*

IKUUA:
> Let me leave now
> For I have to rush to the airport.
> Our friends from America and Germany,
> You know, the ones involved in this factory,
> Arrive at midnight.
> By the way don't worry about the site,
> The peasant whose land adjoins Kīgūunda's
> Has agreed to sell us three acres,
> So that he can buy some shares
> In a land-buying scheme in the Rift Valley
> Of which I am the leader.
> But should Kīgūunda agree to sell his,
> It's alright,
> For the factory will need space for expansion.
> And what did you decide
> About you becoming one of the local directors?
> It's not much work.
> It's just a matter of one or two board meetings.
> You become overseer
> Just as you now oversee their banks.
> You and I will be like watchdogs!
> Holding fleshy bones!

[*He laughs*]

KĪOI:
> It's alright.
> But I think we'd better forward the name of John Mūhūūni.
> Let him become a director,

So that our sons can begin to exercise responsibility!
Charity begins at home.

KIUUA:

So he has come back from Mombasa?

KĪOI:

Yes, and he reported that
All my properties on the coast
Are in good condition.

IKUUA:

Bye, bye.

IKUUA *goes out.* KĪOI *goes on calculating a bit and jotting a few things down. Suddenly there is an urgent knocking at the door. He hides the money. Before he has hidden everything away,* KĪGŪŪNDA *and* WANGECI, *in their old working clothes, enter.*

KĪGŪŪNDA:

We have come
Because something unexpected has happened.
Instead of Wangeci and I marrying in church
The children had better marry first.

KĪOI:

Children?
Which children?

WANGECI:

Mūhūūni and Gathoni.

KĪOI:

John Mūhūūni!
Which Mūhūūni are you talking about?

KĪGŪŪNDA:

Has he not told you?

KĪOI:

What?
Tell me.

KĪGŪŪNDA ⎫
WANGECI ⎬ : That he has made Gathoni pregnant.

KĪOI: [*Very angry*]

My son can't do a thing like that.
We have brought him up in Christian ways . . .

Go away from here.
I don't want to hear any nonsense from you.
Why are you unable to look after your children?

WANGECI:

Aaa – uuu – u!
We shall go to court.
We are all equal before the law.

KĪOI: [*Smiling*]

Did you say 'court'? Law?
Run. Hurry up.
We shall see on whose side the law is!
Your side or our side!
There are no laws to protect parents
Who are unable to discipline their children,
Who let their children become prostitutes.
I am a mature person,
I've been made mature by Christ.
And I can let my son marry
Only from the home of a mature person.

KĪGŪŪNDA: [*Pulling out the sword*]

So I'm not a human being?
So I have no feelings?
Is that why you dare call my daughter a whore
In my very presence?
Don't you know how it pains
When I truly know that
It's your son who lured her away from home?
Now I'll prove to you that
I am a human being!
This sword is my law and my court.
Poor people's lawcourt.

[KĪOI *is trembling with hands raised*]

You'll die now.
Kneel down.
Kneel!

[KĪOI *kneels down*]

Look at yourself, you Nebuchadnezzar.

You are the one turned into a beast.
Walk on all fours.
Walk on your feet and hands.
[KĪOI *walks on all fours*]
Eat grass,
Christ, the Head, is watching you,
Walk!
[WANGECI *is beseeching* KĪGŪŪNDA *not to kill him*]
WANGECI:
Don't kill him.
Let him sign an agreement.
KĪGŪŪNDA:
This one?
To sign an agreement?
KĪOI:
Yes, I'll sign.
I'll sign anything you want me to sign.
Even if you want them to go to church tonight
They'll go!
KĪGŪŪNDA: [*With pride*]
Church, your churches?
Let me tell you a thing or two Mr Ahab Kīoi.
Even if you were now to give me all the wealth
Which you and your clansmen have stolen from the poor,
Yes, the wealth which you and your Asian and European
    clansmen
And all the rich from Kenya share among yourselves,
I would not take it.
Just now,
No amount of gold or ivory or gemstones
Would make me let Gathoni marry your son.
But as for signing something,
You will!
Earthly debts must be paid here on earth.
It is said the fart of the rich never smells
But yours Kīoi stinks all over the earth.

JEZEBEL *peeps in and quickly rushes back to the inner rooms. The*

SECURICOR WATCHMAN *and* NDUGĪRE *and* HELEN *enter.* KĪGŪŪNDA *is not afraid. But* NDUGĪRE *and* HELEN *are trembling with fear, and they don't seem to know what to do. The* WATCHMAN *takes out his whistle and starts blowing it and threatening* KĪGŪŪNDA *from a safe distance. But whenever* KĪGŪŪNDA *moves a step towards them they all run to an even safer distance.*

KĪGŪŪNDA:

> Wangeci bring a piece of paper from that table.
> I want all these to witness
> Ahab Kīoi wa Kanoru's signature.

The WATCHMAN *goes on blowing his whistle and threatening* KĪGŪŪNDA, *but with his eyes very much on the door. Before* KĪGŪŪNDA *gets the piece of paper,* JEZEBEL *enters with a gun, a pistol. The* WATCHMAN *and the* NDUGĪRES *give way and follow behind her, now all acting brave. With her eyes on* KĪGŪŪNDA'*s sword and pointing the gun at him she walks to where her husband is and helps him to his feet with a hand.* WANGECI *goes to where* KĪGŪŪNDA *is and tries to get the sword from him. But* KĪGŪŪNDA *pushes her away. Now it is the confrontation between the gun and the sword.*

JEZEBEL:

> Put that sword down.

KĪGŪŪNDA *at first refuses, then he reluctantly lets the sword fall to the ground.* JEZEBEL *bends down and pushes away the sword, while still pointing the gun at* KĪGŪŪNDA.

JEZEBEL:

> Get out. Get out of here.

KĪGŪŪNDA *and* WANGECI *start to leave. But at the door,* KĪGŪŪNDA *quickly turns round as if finally determined to regain his sword and fight it out.* JEZEBEL *fires the gun.* KĪGŪŪNDA *falls.*

END OF SCENE TWO

Scene Three

Kīgūūnda's home. About two weeks after. Kīgūūnda is not in. Most of the new things are no longer there. The house is very much like the way

*it was at the beginning of the play, except for the picture of
Nebuchadnezzar and the board with the inscription 'Christ is the
Head' which still hang from the walls as if in mockery. Note that the
board with the inscription, 'Christ is the Head' hangs on the spot where
the title-deed used to hang.* WANGECI *is sitting on a chair, dejected.*
NJOOKI *is standing near her, trying to comfort her.* GĪCAAMBA *is
standing near the board with the inscription, as if he is reading the
letters, shaking his head from side to side in disbelief.*

WANGECI:
    What shall I now do?
    Where shall I now turn?
    Oh, oh, my child!
GĪCAAMBA:
    Where is Gathoni?
WANGECI:
    My friends: don't ask me.
NJOOKI:
    But why? Where is Gathoni?
WANGECI:
    Her father threw her out of the house.
    I stayed for a week without knowing
    Where she had gone.
    Now I hear that she is a barmaid.
    My daughter!
    A barmaid!
    Gathoni my child!
    To become a whore?
GĪCAAMBA: [*Moving away from the board*]
    Let's not call our children prostitutes.
    A hyena is very greedy
    But she does not eat her young.
    Our children are not to blame.
    Gathoni is not to blame.
    When a bird in flight gets very tired
    It lands on the nearest tree.
    We the parents have not put much effort

In the education of our girls.
Even before colonialism,
We oppressed women
Giving ourselves numerous justifications:

[*Sings*]

Women and property are not friends,
Two women are two pots of poison,
Women and the heavens are unpredictable,
Women cannot keep secrets,
A woman's word is believed only after the event.

And through many other similar sayings,
Forgetting that a home belongs to man and woman,
That the country belongs to boys and girls.
Do you think it was only the men
Who fought for Kenya's independence?
How many women died in the forests?
Today when we face problems
We take it out on our wives,
Instead of holding a dialogue
To find ways and means of removing darkness from the land.

[*Sings*]

Come my friend
Come my friend
Let's reason together.
Our hearts are heavy
Over the future of our children.
Let's find ways of driving darkness
From the land.

NJOOKI:
Gathoni now has no job.
She has no other means of earning a living
And she would like to dress up
Like all her age-mates.

WANGECI:
Would she were a housemaid!

NJOOKI:

>A housemaid?
>To be collecting all the shit in somebody else's house?
>And when the memsahib is out of sight,
>The husband wants the maid to act the wife!
>Thus the maid doing all the work for memsahib!

GĪCAAMBA ⎱   [*Sing as if continuing the song*
NJOOKI   ⎰ :   *Gĩcaamba has just sung*]

>>*Yes we find out why*
>>*It's the children of the poor*
>>*Who look after rich people's homes,*
>>*Who serve them beer in beer-halls,*
>>*Who sell them their flesh.*
>>>*Come my friend*
>>>*Come my friend*
>>>*We reason together.*
>>>*Our hearts are heavy*
>>>*Over the future of our children.*
>>>*Let's find ways of driving away darkness*
>>>*From the land.*

WANGECI:

>Oh, my child!

NJOOKI:

>She will come back!
>Our children will one day come back!

GĪCAAMBA:

>And where now is Kĩgũũnda?

WANGECI:

>I don't know!
>He might be in a beer-hall.
>Ever since he lost his job,
>He had become married to Chibuku liquor!
>And now he has lost his piece of land.

GĪCAAMBA ⎱ : What?
NJOOKI   ⎰

WANGECI:

>Didn't you hear about it over the radio?
>You too have forgotten us.

NJOOKI:
>   No!
>   We have not forgotten you,
>   Gĩcaamba has been on night shifts.
>   And again we noticed
>   That since you started friendship with the Kĩois,
>   You did not really want our company.

WANGECI:
>   Nobody repents the sins of another.
>   Nobody regrets the going as the returning.

GĨCAAMBA:
>   What about the piece of land?

WANGECI:
>   We went to Kĩoi's place
>   To tell him about Gathoni and Mũhũũni.
>   Kĩoi and Kĩgũũnda exchanged heated words.
>   Kĩgũũnda took out his sword.
>   Kĩoi's wife took out a gun.

GĨCAAMBA
NJOOKI   } : What? A gun?

WANGECI:
>   What can I say?
>   We are now breathing
>   Only because the bullets missed us
>   Death was not ready to receive us.
>   Kĩoi said he would not pursue the matter further,
>   But he dismissed Kĩgũũnda from his job.

NJOOKI:
>   If only I could catch that Kĩoi.
>   With these hands that know toil
>   I would teach him a thing or two!

WANGECI:
>   After a week
>   Kĩgũũnda got a letter from the bank's lawyers.
>   The letter said: pay back the loan
>   Or we shall sell your piece of land.
>   Kĩgũũnda has no job.
>   He has tried to sell the goods

We foolishly bought with the loan money
And they are not fetching much.
So the radio announced that
The piece of land would be auctioned.

NJOOKI:

We never heard the announcement.
When will it be auctioned?

WANGECI:

Today.
It was being auctioned today.

NJOOKI:

Today?

WANGECI:

Today! This day!
Today was the day
The Kīois buried us alive.

KĪGŪŪNDA'*s drunken voice can be heard. He is singing.*

I shall marry when I want
While all padres are still alive
And I shall get married when I want
While all nuns are still alive.

KĪGŪŪNDA *enters, very drunk.*

KĪGŪŪNDA:

How are you?
Son of Kīhooto,
Why didn't you join me for a drink?
Chibuku for power.
Kill me quick: Chibuku.
You Gīcaamba have become tied
To your wife's apron strings.
Do you suckle her?
Women are useless.
A woman is a pot full of poison.

WANGECI:

And so Chibuku has married you?
Every day. In the morning. In the evening.
Whenever you sell anything

> To get money to pay back the loan,
> You go to a beer-hall where Chibuku is sold.
> Chibuku!
> Chang'aa liquor!
> Poison poured into our country!

GĪCAAMBA:

> Yes, yes, by the whites
> And their local followers.
> Servants to foreigners!

KĪGŪŪNDA: [*Sings and dances*]

> > *Greet Chibuku for me*
> > *Chibuku chased away my bitterness*
> > *Chibuku chased away pain, sorrow and thoughts.*

WANGECI:

> Go away,
> Go back to the beer-halls
> Where your daughter is selling beer
> And dance and sing in there.

KĪGŪŪNDA:

> Shut up, woman!
> Gĩcaamba, never trust a woman.

WANGECI:

> Was I the one who told you
> To go for loans from other people's banks?

KĪGŪŪNDA:

> Who wanted a church wedding?
> You an old woman
> Wanting to go through a humiliating ceremony!
> And all because of looking down upon our culture!
> You saw fools going for foreign customs
> And you followed in their footsteps.
> Do you think that it's only foreign things
> Which are blessed?

WANGECI:

> You are not the one talking.
> It's liquor speaking through you.

KĪGŪŪNDA: [*Worked up*]

You now insult me!
You dare insult me!
Have church weddings entered your brains?

He takes the picture of Nebuchadnezzar and breaks it to pieces. He does the same for the board with the inscription, 'Christ is the Head'.

WANGECI:
Do you think that breaking those
Will bring back the piece of land?

WANGECI *and* KĪGŪŪNDA *fight.* GĪCAAMBA *and* NJOOKI *separate them.*
WANGECI *is crying and shouting all sorts of insults.*

WANGECI:
Kill me!
Let him murder me!
Murder me before the whole population!
Kīoi has proved too much for you.
Chibuku has proved too much for you.
Your daughter has proved too much for you.
O.K., kill me! Kill me now!
Leave him alone, the poor wretch.
Let him now kill me
So he can have meat for supper.

KĪGŪŪNDA *suddenly changes as if a mortal blow had been struck at his own identity. He slumps into a seat, completely dejected, but rapt in thought.* WANGECI *is also dejected as she too takes a seat.*

GĪCAAMBA:
Whatever the weight of our problems,
Let's not fight amongst ourselves.
Let's not turn violence within us against us,
Destroying our homes
While our enemies snore in peace.

KĪGŪŪNDA:
You have spoken the truth.
For from today Kīoi has become my enemy.
Either I die, or he dies.
Why, they have buried me alive!

NJOOKI:
The piece of land . . . was it sold?

KĪGŨŨNDA: [*Pause*]
Yes. [*Shows them his hand*]
Now we have only our hands.

GĪCAAMBA:
Who . . . Who bought it?

KĪGŨŨNDA: [*Pause*]
Ahab Kĩoi wa Kanoru.

NJOOKI:
A-uuu-u!
That man should now be baptized
The Oppressor, Son of Grab-and-Take.

ALL:
The Oppressor, Son of Grab-and-Take.

KĪGŨŨNDA:
When I left the auction place
I thought I should revisit the piece of land
For a last glance,
A kind of goodbye.
Who did I find there?
Kĩoi wa Kanoru, Ikuua wa Nditika
Plus a group of whites.
I fled.
But their open laughter followed me . . .

GĪCAAMBA:
The laughter from the clansmen of . . .

KĪGŨŨNDA
NJOOKI   } : The Oppressor, Son of Grab-and-Take.
WANGECI

*The same group of people who had sung in Act One now come back
and break into the same song.*

> The devil of robbery
> Must be crushed
> Hallelujah let's crush him
> For the second coming is near.
> He has brought famine to this land
> Let's crush him.
> Hallelujah let's crush him
> For the second coming is near.

The devil of oppression
Must be crushed.

The LEADER *of the group enters with a container.*

LEADER:

It's a haraambe to build a church
For those troubled at heart
For those carrying pain in their hearts!

WANGECI *unties a handkerchief and takes out a shilling which she puts into the container. She stands at the door and watches the group as they now sing a hymn of harvest:*

We bring you this offering, oh Lord,
It is the fruit of our toil on the land.
Take it Lord and bless it.
Take it Lord and bless it.

   If you give in a tiny calabash,
   In heaven you'll be paid in a similar container.
   If you give in a big wide basin,
   In heaven you'll be paid in a similar container.
   And if you don't give anything,
   You too will never receive blessings.
   Lord take it and bless it.

We bring you this offering, Oh Lord,
It's the fruit of our toil on the land.
Take it Lord and bless it.
Take it Lord and bless it.

The SINGERS *go away singing.* WANGECI *returns to her seat.* GĨCAAMBA *is shaking his head from side to side.*

GĨCAAMBA:

This has become too much for us.
The Kĩois and the Ikuuas,
For how long will they continue oppressing us?
The European Kĩoi, the Asian Kĩoi,
The African Kĩoi,
What's the difference?
They are clansmen.
They know only how to take from the poor.
When we took the Mau Mau oath,

We used to make this vow:
I'll always help this organization
With all my strength and property
I'll always aid members of this organization.
If a bean falls to the ground
We shall split it equally among us.
If I fail to do so,
May this, the people's oath, destroy me
And the blood of the masses turn against me.

LL: [*They repeat as if renewing a political vow*]

ĪCAAMBA:

Our nation took the wrong turn
When some of us forgot these vows.
They forgot all about the people's movement
And they took over the programme of the homeguards,
They said that a vulture eats alone
That no bird of prey preys for another.
They turned into sucking, grabbing and taking away.
That group is now ready to sell the whole country to foreigners.
Go to any business premise;
Go to any industry;
Go to any company;
Even if you find an African behind the counter,
Smoking a pipe over a protruding belly,
Know that he is only an overseer, a well-fed watchdog,
Ensuring the smooth passage of people's wealth
To Europe and other foreign countries.
Grabbers
Exploiters
Oppressors
Eaters of that which has been produced by others:
Their religion,
Their hymn,
Their prayer
Are all one:
Oh, God in heaven,
Shut the eyes of the poor,

The workers and the peasants
The masses as a whole
Ensure that they never wake up and open their eyes
To see what we are really doing to them!
Wa Gathoni,
We too should think hard,
Let's wake up and reason together, now.

ALL: [*They sing.* WANGECI *stands up and sings facing and looking at* KĪGŪŪNDA. KĪGŪŪNDA *also stands up and walks towards her. They mee and hold hands as they continue singing*]

> Come my friend
> Come my friend
> Let's reason together.
> Our hearts are heavy with worry
> Because of the future of our children.
> Let's drive away the darkness
> From all our land.

GĪCAAMBA:

The question is this:
Who are our friends? And where are they?
Who are our enemies? And where are they?
Let us unite against our enemies.
I don't need to elaborate!
He who has ears, let him hear,
He who has eyes, let him see.
I know only this:
We cannot end poverty by erecting a hundred churches in the
   village:
We cannot end poverty by erecting a hundred beer-halls in the
   village;
Ending up with two alcoholics.
The alcoholic of hard liquor.
The alcoholic of the rosary.
Let's rather unite in patriotic love:
Gĩkũyũ once said:

[*Sings*]

> Two hands can carry a beehive,

        One man's ability is not enough,
        One finger cannot kill a louse,
        Many hands make work light.
Why did Gĩkũyũ say those things?
Development will come from our unity.
Unity is our strength and wealth.
A day will surely come when
If a bean falls to the ground
It'll be split equally among us,
        For —

[*They sing*]

SOLOIST:
    The trumpet —

ALL:
        Of the workers has been blown
        To wake all the slaves
        To wake all the peasants
        To wake all the poor.
        To wake the masses

SOLOIST:
    The trumpet —

ALL:
    Of the poor has been blown.

SOLOIST:
    The trumpet!

ALL:
        The trumpet of the masses has been blown.
        Let's preach to all our friends.
        The trumpet of the masses has been blown.
        We change to new songs
        For the revolution is near.

SOLOIST:
    The trumpet!

ALL:
        The trumpet of the masses has been blown.

SOLOIST:
    The trumpet!

ALL:
> The trumpet of the masses has been blown.
> We are tired of being robbed
> We are tired of exploitation
> We are tired of land grabbing
> We are tired of slavery
> We are tired of charity and abuses.

SOLOIST:
> The trumpet!

ALL:
> The trumpet of the poor has been blown.
> Let's unite and organize
> Organization is our club
> Organization is our sword
> Organization is our gun
> Organization is our shield
> Organization is the way
> Organization is our strength
> Organization is our light
> Organization is our wealth.

SOLOIST:
> The trumpet!

ALL:
> The trumpet of the masses has been blown.

SOLOIST:
> The trumpet —

ALL:
> Of the workers has been blown
> There are two sides in the struggle,
> The side of the exploiters and that of the exploited.
> On which side will you be when

SOLOIST:
> The trumpet —

ALL:
> Of the workers is finally blown?

CURTAIN

APPENDIX:
SONGS IN THE ORIGINAL GĨKŨYŨ

p. 4

Mũrĩu: *Ngaahikania ndeenda*
Mũbia nĩ atũire,
Na ngaahika ndeenda
Wa mwarĩ nĩ atũire!

Ngaahika ndeenda
Mũbia nĩ atũire,
Na ngaahika ndeenda
Wa mwarĩ nĩ atũire!

pp. 5–7

Caitaani wa mathĩĩna
Nĩ araangwo
Harĩrũiya nĩ araangwo,
Na akinyĩrĩrio ihĩinda rĩ hakuhĩ.
Nĩ athũũkagia micĩĩ iitũ
Nĩ araangwo!
Harĩrũiya nĩ araangwo,
Na akinyĩrĩrio ihĩinda rĩ hakuhĩ.
Caitaani wa maũici
Nĩ araangwo!
Harĩrũiya nĩ araangwo,
Na aikinyĩrĩrio ihĩinda rĩ hakuhĩ.
Nĩ araangwo na akorogerwo,
Nĩ araangwo!
Harĩrũiya nĩ araangwo,
Na akinyĩrĩrio ihĩinda rĩ hakuhĩ.
Nĩ athĩĩnagia bũrũri,
Nĩ araangwo!
Harĩrũiya nĩ araangwo,
Na akinyĩrĩrio ihĩinda rĩ hakuhĩ.

Caitaani wa ũtuunyani
Nĩ araangwo!
Harĩrũiya nĩ araangwo,
Na akinyĩrĩrio ihĩinda rĩ hakuhĩ.
Nĩ athikwo ahaandĩrwo itũra
Nĩ araangwo!
Harĩrũiya nĩ araangwo,
Na akinyĩrĩrio ihĩinda rĩ hakuhĩ.
Nĩ ahũũtagia ciana ciitũ,
Nĩ araangwo!
Harĩrũiya nĩ araangwo,
Na akinyĩrĩrio ihĩinda rĩ hakuhĩ.

Caitaani wa ũhinyĩrĩria,
Nĩ araangwo!
Harĩrũiya nĩ araangwo,
Na akinyĩrĩrio ihĩinda rĩ hakuhĩ.
Nĩ akinywo na athimiindĩrwo,
Nĩ araangwo!

Harĩrũiya nĩ araangwo,
Na akinyĩrĩrio ihĩinda rĩ hakuhĩ.
Nĩ agiragia twarahũke,
Nĩ araangwo!
Harĩrũiya nĩ araangwo,
Na akinyĩrĩrio ihĩinda rĩ hakuhĩ.
Andũ aitũ tũine twĩ hamwe,
Nĩ araangwo!
Harĩrũiya nĩ araangwo,
Na akinyĩrĩrio ihĩinda rĩ hakuhĩ.
Nĩ geetha tũkoona ũtheri,
Nĩ araangwo!
Harĩrũiya nĩ araangwo,
Na akinyĩrĩrio ihĩinda rĩ hakuhĩ.
Ndiikũigua mũkĩamũkĩria,
Nĩ araangwo!
Harĩrũiya nĩ araangwo,
Na akinyĩrĩrio ihĩinda rĩ hakuhĩ. . .

p. 8

Caitaani wa aimani,
Nĩ araangwo!
Harĩrũiya nĩ araangwo,
Na akinyĩrĩrio ihĩinda rĩ hakuhĩ.
Nĩ aagiria twake Kanitha,
Nĩ araangwo!

Harĩrũiya nĩ araangwo,
Na akinyĩrĩrio ihĩinda rĩ hakuhĩ.

Caitaani wa nduma-inĩ
Nĩ araangwo. . .

pp. 11–13

(E ta mũkũi)
Nĩ nĩĩ ndoirĩirwo nĩ mbura
Kĩrĩma kĩa mũtĩrĩri,
(Cĩĩgaamba)
Kĩrĩma kĩa mũtĩrĩri
Ngĩambata na ngĩkũrũka!!
Ĩ hũũĩ humae. . .
. . . hae haiya!
Ĩ hũũĩ humae. . .
. . . hae haiya!
Nĩ nĩĩ ndoirĩirwo nĩ mbura
Kĩrĩma kĩa mũtĩrĩri,
Kĩrĩma kĩa mũtĩrĩri
Ngĩambata na ngĩkũrũka!
Ndaatukĩrĩirwo Gĩkũyũ
Hũĩ, kĩrĩrĩ kĩa mbũiya,
(Cĩĩgaamba, ihũũni, mĩrũri)
Maitũ akiuga nĩ njookerwo,
Baaba akiuga ndiicookerwo.
Ĩ hũũĩ humae. . .
. . . hae haiya!
Ĩ hũũĩ humae. . .
. . . hae haiya!
Ndaatukĩrĩirwo Gĩkũyũ

Hũĩ, kĩrĩrĩ kĩa mbũiya,
Maitũ akiuga nĩ njookerwo,
Baaba akiuga ndiicookerwo.
Mũrĩĩtu ngwatia makubu,
Naanii ngũgwatie gũtũũgio!
(Cĩĩgaamba, ihũũni, mĩrũri)
Na gĩtũũgio ngũgũrũũgia
Hũĩ, ũũrie mbaru-ini,
(Cĩĩgaamba)
Wona worira mbaru-inĩ,
Hũĩ ndũgaacooka kuonwo!
Ĩ hũũĩ humae. . .
. . . hae haiya!
Ĩ hũũĩ humae. . .
. . . hae haiya!
Mũrĩĩtu ngwatia makubu
Naanii ngũgwatie gĩtũũgio.
Na gĩtũũgio ngũgũrũũgia.
Hũĩ, ũũrire mbaru-ini.
Wona worira mbaru-ini.
Hũĩ ndũgaacooka kuonwo!
Gũũkũ nĩ kũ ngwanĩrira
Kũũndũ maitũ aareganire.
(Cĩĩgaamba. . .)
Kũũndũ maitũ aareganire,
Naanii ngĩthuguma ũrĩrĩ!
Ĩ hũũĩ humae. . .
. . . hae haiya!
Ĩ hũũĩ humae. . .
. . . hae haiya!
Gũũkũ nĩ kũ ngwanĩrira
Kũũndũ maitũ aareganire
Kũũndũ maitũ aareganire
Naanii ngĩthuguma ũrĩrĩ!

Maitŭ oimire njaŭ ya ita,
(Cĩigaamba. . .)
Yaatuungatĩirwo nĩ aanake,
Yaatuungatĩirwo nĩ aanake,
Kamũingi kooyaga ndĩrĩ
Ĩ hũũĩ humae. . .
. . . hae haiya!
Ĩ hũũĩ humae. . .
. . . hae haiya!
Maitŭ oimire njaŭ ya ita,
Yaatuungatĩirwo nĩ aanake,
Yaatuungatĩirwo nĩ aanake,
Kamũingi kooyaga ndĩrĩ!
Maitŭ yŭŭyŭ njugĩrĩria,
Ndaaga gũkua nĩ ngaataha!
(Cĩigaamba, Ngemi)
Magĩrĩ marĩ kũnene
Ndaaga gũkua nĩ ngaataha!
Ĩ hũũĩ humae. . .
. . . hae haiya!
Ĩ hũũĩ humae. . .
. . . haiya!
Maitŭ yŭŭyŭ njugĩrĩria,
Ndaaga gũkua nĩ ngaataha.
Magĩrĩ marĩ kũnene
Ndaaga gũkua nĩ ngaataha!
Ngeereni ĩtuunywo ahahami
Ĩneengerwo njaamba ĩrĩ hinya!
(Cĩigaamba, Ngemi)
Ĩneengerwo njaamba ĩrĩ hinya,
Ta ĩtuungati cia Kĩmaathi!
Ĩ hũũĩ humae. . .
. . . hae haiya!
Ĩ hũũĩ humae. . .
. . . hae haiya!
Ngeereni ĩtuunywo ahahami,
Ĩneengerwo njaamba ĩrĩ hinya,
Ĩneengerwo njaamba ĩrĩ hinya,
Ta ĩtuungati cia Kĩmaathi!
Ngeereni ĩtuunywo ahahami
Ĩneengerwo njaamba ĩrĩ hinya
Theengerwa njamba ĩrĩ hinya
Ta Kĩgũũnda wa Gathoni. . .
Ĩneengerwo njaamba ĩrĩ hinya

p. 14

Gũũkũ nĩ kwa ũ
Gũũkũ nĩ kwa ũ
Gũũkũ nĩ kwa ũ
Ndĩitemanie ta njaŭ ya mbogo
Hũĩ wainaga.

Gũũkũ nĩ gwaka
Gũũkũ nĩ gwakwa
Gũũkũ nĩ gwakwa
Ndeenda gwĩtemanie ndĩitemanie
Hũĩ, Wainaga.

pp. 23–4

Nyaangwĩcũ ribariba mũcati ĩ
Nyaangwĩcũ ribariba mũcati ĩ
Wa maitŭ uume kĩria uumaga
Wa maitŭ uume kĩria uumaga.

Nyaangwĩcũ nĩ ya kagũrũ kamwe
Nyaangwĩcũ nĩ ya kagũrũ kamwe
Gũũkũ kũũngĩ nĩ gũkenia cĩiga
Gũũkũ kũũngĩ nĩ gũkenia cĩiga.

Wangeci Kairĩitu karũũngarũ
Wangeci Kairĩitu karũũngarũ
Karũũngarũ ta mũtĩ wa mũna
Karũũngarũ ta mũtĩ wa mũna.

Wangeci kairĩitu kaniini
Wangeci kairĩitu kaniini
Ndĩkoonaga ngaremwo nĩ gũthĩĩ
Ndĩkoonaga ngaremwo nĩ gũthĩĩ.

Wangeci tũrimĩre matuunda
Wangeci tũrimĩre matuunda
Maya ma Kĩgũũnda wa Gathoni
Maya ma Kĩgũũnda wa Gathoni.

Wangeci wa maitŭ nĩ twarega ĩ
Wangeci wa maitŭ nĩ twarega ĩ
Gũtũũra twĩ ngoombo mũciĩ witũ
Gũtũũra twĩ ngoombo mũciĩ witũ.

pp. 24–5

Mwomboko ti hinya
No makinya meerĩ na kuuna.
Ngũkuombora meerĩ
Nyũkwa arĩ mũgũũnda
Na thooguo Njoohi-inĩ
Ũunjĩirĩre mbeeti ya thoguo.

Njogekerera
Naaniĩ nguogekerera
Ndeto ithiragĩra itherũ-inĩ.

Gwitũ nĩ Rĩmuuru
Gũũkũ nĩ rũteeki njũkĩĩte
Ĩĩ Wangeci reendi
Kinya ũguo ũkinyĩĩte
Na ndũkoongerere
Mũthĩire.

Njogekerera
Naaniĩ nguogekerera
Ndeto ithiragĩra itherũ-inĩ.

Gũũkũ nĩ kuo kwanyu
Kũria kũganagwo
Marigũ ma njuuru
Gũciara
Ngũkũinĩra ũrĩre
Wahĩtia kũrira
Ũũkuumwo nĩ ngoro wĩiite.

Njogekerera
Naaniĩ nguogekerera
Ndeto ithiragĩra itherũ-inĩ.

Ngũrugĩire Njoohi
Na wangarũrũka
Kĩonje kĩrumaga mũhiũhia
Witũ wa Gathoni
Ciakorire Wacũ mũgũũnda
Nake agĩikara thĩ gũciria.

Njogekerera
Naaniĩ nguogekerera
Ndeto ithiragĩra itherũ-inĩ.

Nĩ kũnyua mũnyuĩte
Kana nĩ kũrĩĩo mũrĩĩtwo
Ndirĩ ũndũ ngũkoiga
Wangeci gatuunda
Miaka ĩtathirĩĩte
Mũgwanja. . .

pp. 25–6

Wĩyaathi
Wĩyaathi
Wĩyaathi bũrũri wa Kĩrĩĩnyaga
Bũrũri wa gĩkeno
Wĩ ĩtuamba na mĩtĩtũ
Kenya nĩ bũrũri wa andũ airũ.

Tũtiũragia gũthaamio
Kana gũrwarwo njeera
Kana gũrwarwo icigĩrĩra
Toondũ tũtigaatiga

Gûtetera ithaka
Kenya nî bûrûri wa andû airû.

pp. 26–7

Hooyaai ma
Thaithaai ma

Nî amu Ngai no ûria wa tene.
Mûrîîtu ûmwe nî aakuire
Nî ûndû wa kûnyariirwo
Nî ûndû aaregire kwendia bûrûri.

Hooyai ma
Thaithaai ma
Nî amu Ngai no ûria wa tene.

Wendani ndoonire kuo
Wa ciana na atumia
Mbooco yaagwa thî makeenyûrana.
Hooyaai ma
Thaithaai ma
Nî amu Ngai no ûria wa tene.

p. 28

Nî ya marûûri matatû
Haicia beendera
Ngirini nî yo thî iitû
Haicia beendera
Mûtuune thakame iitû
Haicia beendera
Wa mûirû nî mûûndû mûirû
Haicia beendera

Ngeithirio ituungati ciitû

Mooklire kû?
Mooklire kû?
Mooklire kû?
Mooklire njîra ya Wainyahoro,
Makîraarîrîra kwa Waiyaki,
Na ûmenye ti eega
Mbûrîra yaake yaathiire kû?
Ituungati ciitû nî imenyererwo
Itikaae gwikwo ta Waiyaki.
Na ituungati cia Kîmaathi itirî itherû,
Mooklire kû?

pp. 38–9

Haiya, Reke ngwîre,
Nî amu gûtirî ûciaragwo arî mûûgî
Kwa ûguo o na aakorwo ni njûûî nî kwerirwo
'Ndithûire mûûnyoni ta mûûnyanîrîri'
Nî ngûina kimwe,
Toondû nî gûcuukagwo ûteegûteeo.

Thie rîmwe!
Nî tûkîrûîra wiyaathi
Ndooi kabogo tûgaakamaga iria rîa ngirîndi.
Tene ndaariîaga managu
Na rîu no mo ndîîaga.

pp. 41–2

Î gûûkû kwa wa Gathoni î
Ngûraara na ndiinde
Î ngaiyîrwo na marûa.
Î gûûkû kwa. . .
. . . wa Gathoni.
Î ngûraara. . .
. . . na ndiinde
Î ngaiyîrwo na marûa.
Î ngwaria cia aruti-a-wira

Î na arîmi-anyiinyi
Mari nduundu matiûraga.
Î ngwaria cia. . .
. . . aruti-a-wira,
Î na arîmi. . .
. . . anyiinyi,
Mari nduundu matiûraga.
Î ageni mari Kenya î
Marutîrwo mîrigo
Eene mûcii meegûkinya.
Î ageni. . .
. . . mari Kenya
Î marutîrwo. . .
. . . Mîrigo
Eene mûcii meegûkinya.
Ndirithagia baaba î
Na rûthaanju rwa iregi
Î tûgîthiî kûgîrima.
Î ndirithagia. . .
. . . baaba.
Î na rûthaanju. . .
. . . Rwa iregi,
Î tûgîthiî kûgîrima!

p. 46

Nî ngaagûtua mûtegi andû,
Mûtegi andû, mûtegi andû,
Nî ngaagûtua mûtegi andû,
  Wanûmirîra,
  Wanûmirîra,
  Wanûmirîra,
Nî ngaagûtwa mûtegi andû,
  Wanûmirîra.

p. 47

Nî tûgûûkûgooca
Yesû gatûrûme ka Ngai
Yesû thakame yaaku
Îitheragia
  Ndaakûgooca Mwathani.
  Tukuteenderesa, Yesu.
  Yesu Mwana gwendiga:
  Omusaigwo gunazi'za.
  Nkwebaza. Mulokozi
  Nebaza eyanunula nze;
  Eyamponya wa kisa!
  Yesu ankumaansanyusaeta.
  Bulija Yesu yebazibwe.

p. 47

Ngûkinyûkia o kahora,
Njerekeire ya matu-ini
Na nî njûûî nî ngaakinya
Ngahuurûke na aria atheru.

Nî wega Ngai mûtoongoria
Naake Njîîcû nî mûgate
Roho waku mûûnyootokia
Ndikaahiûta kana nyoote.

Nyamû njûru na mîrimû
O na thîîna itiingîînyiita
Cionaga ngiakana mwaki
Nî kûhuumbwo riiri wa Ngai.

p. 49

Rîria Jesu agacooka
Aiyire managî
Na managî nî mo andû
Aria aanakûûra.

Magaathera ta njata
O ta ya Kîwarî!

No guo magaathakara
Managĩ maake.
Twana tũũtũ, twana tũũtũ. . .

p. 57

Mbũri na ng'oombe na mbia!
Itiri na bata
Kĩĩndũ kĩria kĩ na bata
No riiri wa Njĩĩcũ.

Ngũĩkia riĩtho,
Ngaĩkia rĩĩngĩ
Ngoona mwaki
Ũrĩ gwa caitaani
Ngooria nĩ kĩ
Kĩĩngĩtũma!
Ndĩweherere.

p. 58

Ĩtĩkia Ngai, ũtigane na thĩĩna,
Nĩ arĩkuonagia maũũndũ meega.
Akwehererie moothe maria mooru,
Ũgie na igai nĩ ũndũ wa Njĩĩcũ,
  Ĩtĩkia Ngai,
  Ĩtĩkia Ngai,
  Ĩtĩkia Ngai,
  Na ũmwĩhoke we.

p. 59

Ndĩrĩ hĩĩndĩ ngeendia bũrũri
Kana nyone mbeeca irĩ njerũ
Ta Warũhiũ mari na Ruka. . .

p. 60

O na riu maaĩ no marũrũ,
Kuuma miciĩ nginya mawĩra-inĩ
Kuuma ciana nginya andũ agima,
Nĩ marũrũ, tũũkũnyua kĩĩ?

Wathiĩ wabici ũkĩenda ũteithio,
Ũgakora mũũndũ nĩ mũraakaru,
Woiga ũtoonye agakwĩra ndĩ "busy"
Toondũ maaĩ nĩ marũrũ.

O na riu maaĩ no marũrũ
Kuuma miciĩ nginya mawĩra-inĩ
Kuunda Njĩĩcũ na nĩ ũũkũnyootoka,
Toondũ maaĩ nĩ marũrũ

pp. 60–1

Thĩ ĩno ti yaakwa
Nĩ kwĩhĩtũkĩra,
Ikeno ciakwa ciothe,
Igũrũ matu-inĩ
Kũria andũ aingĩ
Meethĩĩrĩire tene,
Na ndĩngĩciria
Ũhoro wa mũciĩ ũrĩ thĩ.

pp. 65–6

Aagacikũ: Ta rekeeĩ nyeendie Njooki maitũ.
  Njooki ndoigire ndĩkaamwendia
  Mĩroongo ya mũũndũ.
Oothe: *(Kũruma)*
Aagacikũ: Ndĩĩmwendagia mĩroongo ya nyaanja.
  Ta nĩ neengero ũũkĩ wakwa,
  Ũũkĩ wakwa ndaaringĩire theenge.
Oothe: *(Kũruma)*

Aagacikũ: Ũũkĩ ũcio ndĩigaga
  Mĩtwe-inĩ ya ĩrĩrĩ
  Ndaakomakoma ngacũna.
Oothe: *(Kũruma)*
Aagacikũ: Nĩ kĩo ndoigire
  Ndikaamwendia mĩroongo
  Toondũ ndaamwendia,
  Indo cia kũria ndiicookerio.
  Ndĩĩmwendagia mĩroongo ya nyaanja.
Oothe: *(Kũruma)*
Aagacikũ: Hũũũũ ngiuga ngaamũtwara
  Gwa Gĩcaamba mũũrũ wa Kĩhooto
  Kũria ũũkĩ ũigagwo na iheembe.
Oothe: *(Ngemi)*
Aagacikũ: Ũcio nĩ Njooki maitũ ndĩreendia
  Kũria ũũkĩ ũigagwo na iheembe,
  Rũkũri rwa mbura igĩrĩ,
  Makaari matatũ irĩĩti-inĩ cia kũraaya.
Oothe: *(Ngemi na kũruma).*
Aagacikũ: Ũhũũ mũka ũrĩ thenya gatagatĩ.
  Ndĩ o njĩra no ngũũka kwa mũgaacikũ,
  Ngĩcaria Njooki maitũ.
Oothe: *(Kũruma)*
Aambũi: Toondũ njũũragia mũgĩĩmbĩ ngaaruta kũ
  Wa kũhũũra igaanjo
  Hũũũũ ngwigiritia kwerũ,
  Harĩa njirũ ya Mũũmbũi,
  Ĩigiritagia guoya.
Oothe: *(Kũruma, ngemi)*
Aambũi: Mũka ũrĩ njikũ ndirĩ kĩĩndũ ĩingĩaga
  No anga kĩria ũtaangĩĩtia
  Kana kĩria giathiire na coomba.
  Naanĩĩ ũũkĩ waku ndĩ na guo.
  Nĩ hũũtĩĩ na ndĩihooya!
Oothe: *(Kũruma)*
Aambũi: Neengererio Njooki maitũ
  Na igũrũ rĩa thoome.
  No ũũkũneengera ndũũma yaakwa,
  Mũka ũrĩ njikũ, ya gũthiinga kĩng'ethũ.
Oothe: *(Kũruma)*
Aambũu: Amu mũcibi no ndĩĩnyiitĩĩtie wa mũka
  Ũrĩ mbũĩ ta mũrathi ng'oombe,
  Na mũcibi wakira ndoigire
  Ngoohorera kwa nyina wa Njooki.
Oothe: *(Kũruma)*
Aagacikũ: Ũcũrũ nĩ guo ũyũ mũka ũrĩ mbũi,
  Wetagĩrĩre ageni,
  Naawe ũũneengere ũũkĩ wakwa,
  Wa mũruru na hang'i na mbakĩ,
  Cia nyoko ĩrĩ njikũ,
  Na ndũũma ndĩ na yo nyarari ĩrĩ njikũ
  Hĩu na irigũ rĩa mũraaru.
Oothe: *(Kũruma, ngemi)*
Aagacikũ: *(Moige ngemi inya cia Kairĩĩtu. Na o Aambũi moige ngemi ithaano cia Kahĩĩ)*
Aagacikũ: Nĩ mwaigua nĩ twendia Njooki riu
  Kwa mbarĩ ĩ ngumo ya mbũi.
  Tũcooke na thuutha tũkarĩme
  Tũrore kana nĩ tũũkuona
  Ng'ũndũ ciitũ ciathiire na ngeretha.
Oothe: *(Kũruma)*
Aambũi: Tũnyiitane mooko meeri.
  Tũrore kana twatooria
  Thũ ciitũ cia bũrũri.
  Bũrũri ũyũ mwega wa Kĩrĩĩnyaga.

* * * * *

p. 67

Ĩĩ tu ĩĩ mee
Mwakua
Mwakorwo nĩ mbũri cia kĩbũi
Irĩ rũgaambi ĩ.
Kũĩ kwĩ mbũri itagũraga
Ndũũhi ndũũhi ici ĩ

Rūbiū, rūbiū,
Mwakua mwakorwo nī mbūri
Cia Gīcikū irī rūgaambi-ī
Kaī kwī mbūri itagūraga,
Ndūūhi ndūūhi ici-ī.

Kũũngũ mbũri ciitũ-ĩ
Kũũngũ ciitũ-ĩ mũhiki witũ-ĩ
Wagũtũtahagĩra maaĩ-ĩ,
Na aarega tũkamũcuuka-cuka cuukũ
Kũũngũ mbũri ciitũ ĩĩ.

Mũũmbũraga kũ
Mũũmbũraga kũ
Ndĩ na biindũki mĩrĩma-inĩ*
Toondũ mũrari waiyũra itara,
Ndĩ na biindũki mĩrĩma-inĩ.

Gũũkũ nĩ kwa ũ
Gũũkũ nĩ kwa ũ
Ndĩ na biindũki mĩrĩma-inĩ
Ndĩitemanie ta njaũ ya mbogo
Ndĩ na biindũki mĩrĩma-inĩ.
Maitũ njugĩra (ngemi)
Maitũ njugĩra (ngemi)
Ndĩ na biindũki mĩrĩma-inĩ
Ndoigĩrwo mbu nĩ mũka wa coomba
Ndĩ na biindũki mĩrĩma-inĩ. (ngemi)

p. 70

Twaathiiaga tũkeneete,
Tũgacooka tũkeneete,
Rũgeendo rwitũ rwarĩ rũega
Tũgĩthiĩ na tũgĩcooka.

Na twakinya rũũĩ Rũirũ
Tũgĩkora rũtyũrĩĩte
Warũingĩ akiuga twake ndaraca
Gũtirĩ wa Iregi ũtũire.

Twathiaathia haniini
Tũgĩkora kamwendia andũ
Gakiuga nĩ geekuuga mbu
Warũingĩ akiuga karekwo koige
Koigithanio na njirũũngi.

Riria Kimaathi witũ aambatire
Kirima-ini ari wiki,
Nĩ eetirie hinya na ũũmĩrĩru
Wa kũhoota Nyakeerũ.

Tũũkũrĩra toondũ tũri andũ airũ
Na tũtirĩ a nyakeerũ
Na tũtirĩ a Mũhĩrĩga wao
Ngai witũ ari mbere.

p. 82

Nvoota wa maũũndũ ma thĩ ino
Nĩ toro na gĩkuũ kĩa muoyo
Kaira rĩĩtwa ria Ngai
Na nĩ eegũkũhonokia.

Mũoyo mũoyo
Mũoyo wa tene na tene,
Ndũri hĩĩndĩ ũkaanyoota
O rĩ kana ri.
Ndũri hĩĩndĩ ũkaanyoota o rĩ.

p. 83

Ũhoro wa gũkena
Nĩ ũũkũĩte gũũkũ gwitũ
Ũhoro mwega nĩ ũyũ
Wa mũhonokia witũ.
Ũhoro nĩ ũũkũĩte
Gũtwĩra o ithuĩ oothe
Ũria oohanagĩra
Na ũria twendeetwo nĩ we.

Kieendo nĩ kinene
Kĩa Njĩĩcũ mũteithania,
Nĩ oimire igũrũ
Nĩ gũtũigũira tha.

Kinya kũgaathwo gwake
Gũkainwo o kũ na kũ
Na mĩhĩriga yoothe
Ĩgaatiga waganu.

p. 93

Ũhoro wa mũoyo
Nĩ wa Mwathani Njĩĩcũ.
Niingĩ nĩ wa hinya ma,
Gũtũtoongoragia.

Na maũũndũ mooru
Maangĩtũkũhĩhĩria
Njĩĩcũ nĩ we mũhoti
Wa gũtũgitĩra.

Matukũ maathira
Ma gũtũũra gũũkũ thĩ,
Tũgaatũũra na Njĩĩcũ
Tene o na Tene.

p. 94

Kĩhikanio kĩa mbere,
Ngai nĩ aaraathimire
Aandamu na Hawa.

O na rĩu no araathimaga
Kĩhikanio githeru,
Hĩĩndĩ iria Akiricitiano
Meekũhikania.

Na thuutha-inĩ makaambata,
Mwathani aatũĩyĩra,
Maambatanie na Kanitha,
Mũhiki wa Kiriicitũ.

p. 95

Njĩĩcũ mũtharaba wakwa
Riu ni ndeeigĩrĩra,
Hĩkĩre, Mwathani wakwa,
O na angĩ maamũtiga.

Mũraata, naawe hanyũka,
Na wihuumbe wĩtĩkio;
Nĩ guo ũgaakinya igũrũ
Gĩkeno-inĩ kwa Ngai.

p. 105

Aka na ng'ombe itirĩ ndũgũ
Aka eerĩ nĩ nyũũngũ igĩrĩ cia ũrogi
Aka na igũrũ matimenyagĩrwo
Aka matirĩ cia ndĩĩro no cia nyiniko
Cia aka ciĩtĩkagio ciaraara.

Ũka mũraata

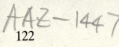

Ũka mũraata
Twaranirie, rĩu
Tũri na kĩeha
Nĩ ũndũ wa ciana
Bũrũri witũ
Ũthire nduma.

p. 106

Ũka mũraata
Twĩciirie nĩ kĩĩ
Ciana cia athĩini
Kũrorera ndoonga micii
Na kũmeenderia njoohi mbaa-inĩ
Na rĩĩrĩ rĩĩngĩ mũrĩ yaao.

Ũka mũraata
Ũka mũraata
Twaranirie, rĩu
Tũri na kĩeha
Nĩ ũndũ wa ciana
Bũrũri witũ
Ũthire nduma.

p. 108

Ngaahikania ndeenda
Mũbia nĩ atũire.
Na ngaahika ndeenda
Wamwari nĩ atũire.

p. 109

Ũngeithirie cibuku
Nĩ we wanyingatĩire kĩrũrũ.
Cibuku nĩ wanjehereirie
Ruo, thĩina, na meeciiria.

pp. 111–12

Caitaani wa ũtuunyani
Nĩ araangwo
Harĩrũiya nĩ araangwo
Na akinyĩrĩrio ihiinda rĩ hakuhĩ.

Nĩ ahũũtagia bũrũri
Nĩ araangwo.
Harĩrũiya nĩ araangwo
Na akinyĩrĩrio ihiinda rĩ hakuhĩ.

Caitaani wa ũhinyĩrĩria
Nĩ araangwo. . .
(O ũguo)

p. 112

Twarehe matega mbere yaku we Mwathani,
Nĩ thithino ya migũünda iitũ tũraagũtegera.
Mwathani mooe na ũmaraathime.
Mwathani mooe na ũmaraathime.

Waheeana na kameni ũkaagaĩrũo o na ko
Mwathani mooe na ũmaraathime.
Waheeana na gũtĩrĩra mũigana na ũcio
Mwathani mooe na ũmaraathime.
Warega gũkĩheeana nĩ anga ũgaakĩiguĩrwo tha,
Mwathani mooe na ũmaraathime.

Twarehe matega mbere yaku we Mwathani,
Nĩ thithino ya migũünda iitũ tũraagũtegera.
Mwathani mooe na ũmaraathime.
Mwathani mooe na ũmaraathime.

p. 114

Ũka mũraata
Ũka mũraata

Twaranirie rĩu
Tũri na kĩeha,
Nĩ ũndũ wa ciana,
Bũrũri witũ.
Ũthire nduma.

pp. 114–15

Thegere igĩrĩ itiremagwo nĩ mwatũ.
Ũũgĩ wa mũũndũ ũmwe ndũrimaga.
Rwambo rũmwe rũtiambaga ndaarwa.
Rũtuungu rũmwe rũtiraaragia mwaki.
Kiara kĩmwe gĩtiũragaga ndaa.
Kamũingĩ kooyaga ndirĩ.

pp. 115–16

Coro
Wa aruti wira nĩ mũhuuhe
Nduungata ciothe twarahũke
Arimi oothe twarahũke
Athĩini oothe twarahũke.

Coro
Coro wa athĩini nĩ mũhuuhe
Coro!
Coro wa athĩini nĩ mũhuuhe,
Tũhuunjĩrie araata aitũ
Coro wa athĩini nĩ mũhuuhe
Tũgarũrire nyĩimbo ciitũ
Nĩ amu ituĩka rĩ hakuhĩ.

Coro!
Coro wa athĩini nĩ mũhuuhe
Coro!
Coro wa athĩini nĩ mũhuuhe
Nĩ tũnogeetio nĩ ũtuunyani
Nĩ tũnogeetio nĩ ũhahami
Ũhahami wa migũünda
Utajiri na ũkombo
O na ũhooi na ũrumani.
Coro!
Coro wa athĩini nĩ mũhuuhe,
Tũnyiitane ngwataniro
Ta ya gikwa na mũkũngũgũ
Ngwataniro nĩ yo njũgũma
Ngwataniro nĩ yo rũhiũ
Ngwataniro nĩ yo mũciinga
Ngwataniro nĩ yo ngo iitũ
Ngwataniro nĩ yo njira
Ngwataniro nĩ you hinya
Ngwataniro nĩ yo ũtheri
Ngwataniro nĩ yo ũtoonga.
Coro!
Coro wa athĩini nĩ mũhuuhe
Coro!
Wa aruti a wira nĩ mũhuuhe
Ngwataniro nĩ igiri
Ya aruti a wira na ya itoonga
Wee ũguakorwo wĩ mwena ũrikũ

Coro!
Wa aruti a wira wahuuhwo!